W9-APJ-784

CASTLES
OF THE
CELTIC LANDS

THE HISTORIC CASTLES OF IRELAND, SCOTLAND AND WALES

CASTLES
OF THE
CELTIC LANDS
THE HISTORIC CASTLES OF
IRELAND, SCOTLAND AND WALES

by Rodney Castleden

BARNES
& NOBLE
NEW YORK

This edition published by Barnes & Noble, Inc., by
arrangement with Smith-Davies Publishing Ltd

2006 Barnes & Noble Books

Copyright © Smith-Davies Publishing Ltd 2006

M 10 9 8 7 6 5 4 3 2 1

ISBN 0-7607-7937-6

All rights reserved. No part of this publication may be reproduced, stored in a retrieval system, or
transmitted in any form or by any means, electronic, mechanical, photocopying, recording or
otherwise, without the prior permission in writing of the copyright owners.

Printed in Singapore

PICTURE ACKNOWLEDGEMENTS
The images on the cover and inside pages were all kindly provided by Alamy Limited, with the
exception of those on p.125, which was supplied by Corbis, and p.129, which was supplied by Irma
Hale.

The image that appears on pages 158–9 is Eilean Donan Castle, Ross-shire.

CONTENTS

INTRODUCTION

Choosing a title was one of the most difficult aspects of writing this book. *Castles of Scotland, Ireland and Wales* would have been accurate but far too cumbersome and, because the West and North of the British Isles are thought of as Celtic, *Celtic Castles* seemed a natural alternative as well as a neat pairing with the title of the companion book, *English Castles*. But using the word 'Celtic' has become increasingly questionable. People living in the North and West of these islands were in the nineteenth century thought of as Celts, a distinct *race* of people who migrated to Britain from central Europe in three waves between 700 and 100 BC, bringing three distinctive cultures with them. It now turns out that none of this is true. The cultural changes that show up in archaeology can be explained by changing fashions; the people were the same people, or descendants of the same people, residing in the British Isles. Recent scholarship shows that the idea of a distinct Western British Celtic race was first put forward in the eighteenth century, with the specific intention of supporting nationalist movements in those areas. So the racial hypothesis was really politically motivated.

Analysis of culture, archaeology and anthropology shows that the 'Celtic' regions of the North and West of the British Isles are in fact very diverse and not particularly related to each other. It turns out that many people who think they are Celtic (for example, 'Welsh') are actually (on grounds of bone structure, DNA or even recent and traceable family history) Anglo-Saxon.

It also turns out that many people living in England who think they are Anglo-Saxon (or 'English') are actually (on the same evidence, where available) of British stock; that is to say that they are descended from people who were already in these islands before the Anglo-Saxon colonization. There is a similar confusion in Lowland Scotland, which was colonized by Anglo-Saxon incomers

Trim Castle, the largest Anglo-Norman castle in Ireland, was constructed over a thirty-year period by Hugh de Lacy and his son Walter.

before Devon and Cornwall were colonized. On that basis it is likely that a greater proportion of the inhabitants of Devon and Cornwall are 'Celtic' (of pre-Anglo-Saxon British stock) than would be the case in Lowland Scotland.

The campaign for a Celtic race petered out in the 1930s when Nazism made racist arguments distasteful. It was discreetly replaced by a substitute campaign for a Celtic culture. This can be argued to have some identity, and it is possible to cobble together a list of superficial but readily identifiable cultural attributes that distinguish 'Welshness', but the colour and texture of this Celtic culture is very modern. Welsh national dress, for instance, is a completely made-up thing with no history at all. When you look closely at it, Welsh culture vanishes.

A big problem, overall, is that the word 'Celtic' is being used as a lever for political advantage, most conspicuously as a way of justifying favours such as devolution. The reality is that Ireland, Scotland, Wales and England are addresses, the people who live there are very diverse, and many of them are not really who they think they are!

Even if a race of Celts and a thorough-going Celtic culture existed, we would still have a problem in referring to Celtic Castles. As will emerge during the course of this book, many of the castles built in Wales, and some in Ireland too, were built and used by Anglo-Norman (or 'English') aristocrats to intimidate and suppress the Welsh and the Irish and were therefore no more Celtic than the concentration camps were Jewish.

In the end, to avoid a long-winded and perhaps evasive-sounding title such as *Castles round the Irish Sea*, we have settled for a compromise title, *Castles of the Celtic Lands*.

And this is just a foretaste of the complex history of these castles of the North and West. Today we see castles as picturesque relics of a romantic past, as left-overs from the chivalry of the middle ages. But they were not seen in that way when they were built – they were symbols of domination and tyranny. At the time they were seen as symbols of raw power, both by the kings and barons who built them and by the ordinary people they were meant to intimidate. Castles were hated by ordinary people because they associated them with oppression and extortion; they were expensive to build and maintain and the cost fell upon ordinary people.

They speak of several different levels of struggle for supremacy. Some were built by knights or lords to show their social superiority over the common people around them. Some were built by barons engaging in wars with one another, wars for status and territory. Some were built by kings struggling to weld a nation by limiting the power of insubordinate barons. Some were built by monarchs exerting supremacy over other nations. The cathedrals and abbeys built at the same time on the same scale were also enmeshed in the contest for status, as is apparent at Kirkwall and St Andrews.

The castles of these lands are incredibly varied, from the very small, like Craigievar, to the enormous, like Caerphilly; from the built-all-at-once, like Borthwick, to the gradually evolving, like Fyvie and Kilchurn; from the obscure, like Claypotts, to the internationally famous, like Harlech and Edinburgh; from those with action-packed histories, like Stirling and Pembroke, to those where nothing at all happened, like Manorbier and Beaumaris. Above all, the stories of these great buildings are inextricably intertwined with the history of the islands, and they give their own distinct perspectives on that history. Caerlaverock is indissolubly linked with Border fighting, Cashel with the career of King Brian Boru, Clifden with the Irish potato famine, Slains and Dunluce with the Spanish Armada, Tintern with the Black Death, Eilean Donan with the end of the Lordship of the Isles, Caerphilly with the fall of Edward II, Braemar with the Jacobite rebellions, Glamis with the life of the Queen Mother.

These wonderfully varied buildings are for many of us our major link to the complex events of a distinctive period of the past – and powerful touchstones to the imagination.

DUNLUCE CASTLE

COUNTY ANTRIM

The ruins of Dunluce Castle have a desolate grandeur, rising melodramatically from a basalt cliff, which in turn looms out of the sea. The castle rock, which is separated from the mainland by a deep natural chasm, occupied a position of profound strategic importance. It was fought over repeatedly until in the sixteenth century it became the main stronghold of the McDonnells.

Dunluce was probably in use as a defensive site 2,000 years ago. A souterrain, an underground storage tunnel or refuge, survives from this early period under the ruins of the later castle. The first stone castle was built in the thirteenth century by Richard de Burgh. The earliest surviving features of the stone castle are the two big round towers 9m (29.5ft) in diameter on the east side. These are remnants of the castle built in the fourteenth century by the McQuillans after they became lords of 'The Route', as the area was known.

Most of the stonework represents the remains of the castle built by Sorley Boy McDonnell, who was born in 1505 and lived to the age of 84. Dunluce was seized by Sorley Boy in 1558 after the death of his brother Colla, who had married the daughter of the McQuillan chief in 1544. Sorley Boy was evicted by Shane O'Neill in 1565 and again in 1584 by Sir John Perrott, but he managed to regain possession with the aid of artillery. He was officially appointed Constable of Dunluce by Queen Elizabeth in 1586.

Repairs to the castle were needed on the landward side, and new work included the addition of a gatehouse with turrets in the Scottish style. Cannon ports in the curtain wall were evidently added to make use of the four cannons taken from the Girona, a galliass from the Spanish Armada which was wrecked nearby, on Lacada Point at the Giant's Causeway. A very unusual feature is the north-facing Italian-style loggia installed behind the curtain wall in the 1560s. This feature was copied from Scottish castles, but it was later blocked, in 1636, by the building of a lavish three-storey gabled house for Lady Catherine MacDonnell, wife of Randal MacDonnell, the second Earl of Antrim.

Inventories show that this house had magnificent furnishings, including cast-off curtains from Cardinal Wolsey's Hampton Court Palace. Lady Catherine had big ideas – she was after all the widow of the assassinated Duke of Buckingham. She may have been responsible for the creation of the mainland court, which was built to replace the lower yard when some of its domestic buildings, including the kitchen, fell into the sea along with most of the servants in 1639.

The Earl and Countess of Antrim lived in great style, frequently attending Charles I's court in London, where they picked up most of their furnishings.

The second Earl was a Royalist, and was arrested by Parliamentarian troops at Dunluce in 1642. After that the family stopped living at Dunluce Castle, which gradually slid into decay. The ruined castle remained the property of the Earls of Antrim until 1928, when it was handed over to the state for preservation.

CLIFDEN CASTLE

COUNTY GALWAY

Clifden Castle in Connemara was built by John D'Arcy in the early nineteenth century. It was a modest castle, a miniature masterpiece in Gothic Revival style. John D'Arcy was a man of considerable determination and energy, founding Clifden town as well as the castle. He founded the town in 1812, and built his castle there, for his own use, at about the same time.

Mr D'Arcy had fourteen children by two successive wives, so the castle must have been a very full and lively family home.

John D'Arcy died in 1839, leaving both the castle and the town to his eldest son, Hyacinth D'Arcy. But these were difficult times in the West of Ireland and it was a bitter legacy that Hyacinth was left. The Great Famine of the 1840s caused misery throughout the community. The poor starved and the landowners could not expect any rent from them. The famine caused Hyacinth D'Arcy to run up huge debts and, like a great many other landlords of the time in the West of Ireland, he went bankrupt. In 1850, both the town and the castle were up for sale. Hyacinth D'Arcy lost them.

The new owners of Clifden Castle were the Eyre family from Bath in England. They bought the town and castle for £21,245 and lived in the castle until the 1920s. Then the properties were bought by the State and divided up among the tenants. The castle unfortunately ended up with no outright owner and as a result nobody maintained it and it fell into neglect. It then suffered the fate of many another castle in earlier centuries, becoming a quarry for building materials. The slates were taken from the roof, the timbers were robbed out and Clifden Castle quickly became a modern ruin.

One curious feature of Clifden is the standing stones. D'Arcy had them raised to mimic the ancient megalithic monuments of Ireland. D'Arcy liked to pretend they were ancient, but they are not.

The masonry shell of the castle is in a surprisingly good state of preservation. It is possible to walk inside the house by way of an entrance through the back garden. It is no longer possible to enter from the front because of a steep drop into the structure; it is in any case inadvisable to explore ruined buildings without advice from local people who know whether they are safe or not.

At first glance, on approaching it, Clifden Castle appears intact. It is only when you notice that there is no glass in any of the windows that you realize that Clifden is derelict. It is a sad end to a fine house.

Clifden Castle was founded at the start of the ninteenth century by John d'Arcy. The Castle is now a roofless ruin on the scenic Sky Road running westwards along Clifden Bay.

MELLIFONT ABBEY

COUNTY LOUTH

In 1140, Malachy, the former Archbishop of Armagh, went on a pilgrimage to Rome with some disciples. On his way to and from Rome he visited Clairvaux, where he met the great St Bernard. He was so impressed that he wanted to set up a community in Ireland on the Clairvaux model. Bernard kept four of Malachy's disciples for training and asked Malachy to find a suitable place. He eventually found an isolated spot on the River Mattock, not far from Drogheda. It was in the territory of King Donnchadh of Airghialla, who supported the religious reform movement. The king gave the land to the Cistercian Order and the first monks arrived from Clairvaux to set up the abbey. One of the French arrivals was Robert, the abbey's architect. Malachy was distraught when Bernard recalled him before the building work was finished.

In 1152, the new Mellifont Abbey hosted the Synod of Drogheda, though the abbey church was not consecrated until five years later. Mellifont grew and grew in importance, and by the end of the twelfth century it had spawned 23 daughter houses. The arrival of the Anglo-Normans in Ireland in 1169 created friction in the Irish Cistercian houses. The first Abbot of Mellifont, Giolla Criost, welcomed these newcomers, but the monks ousted a later pro-Norman abbot. Then Abbot Thomas ordered the monastery doors closed to visitors. Thomas was deposed, but the rebellion, which spread to other Cistercian monasteries in Ireland, became known on the Continent as 'the Mellifont Conspiracy'.

Mellifont Abbey declined in the fourteenth and fifteenth centuries. In 1471, the Chapter General took action against Mellifont as it was on the verge of ruin. Abbot John Troy launched a series of reforms, but his successor let things go again – and then the Reformation overtook the abbey in 1539. It is said that a small group of monks stayed on, and the title 'Abbot of Mellifont' continued in use for a long time after the Dissolution. When war broke out in 1641, the Cistercians began to disperse. In 1718, the last Cistercian Abbot of Mellifont died.

The Irish Cistercians returned to Ireland in 1831, when the French expelled all British subjects (which then still included Irish). They did not return to Mellifont at once, and it was only a hundred years later that they managed to purchase Mellifont Abbey. The Cistercians founded a new monastery there and in 1945 it became an abbey once more – and known as Mellifont Abbey.

The visible remains at Mellifont are not the original twelfth century buildings. The later church was 60m (197ft) long and 20m (65.5ft) wide. The outlines of the earlier church can be discerned in the chancel and transepts, which were extended in the rebuilding. The Abbey church has a unique crypt at its west end. This was probably designed to give the building structural support. Some have suggested that the crypt was a prison, but there is no hard evidence as to its purpose. When the church was rebuilt in the fourteenth century, the mysterious crypt too was rebuilt.

TRIM CASTLE

COUNTY MEATH

Just three years after the Anglo-Normans invaded Ireland, a Norman magnate called Hugh de Lacy built a round motte (an artificial castle mound) with a timber tower on top. This was the first fortification to be built at Trim, in 1173. It was the first step in the Anglo-Norman conquest of County Meath. Rory O'Connor, King of Connaught and last High King of Ireland, recognized the significance of the building, felt threatened by its presence and assembled an army to destroy it. The constable in charge, Hugh Tyrell, set fire to the timber castle and abandoned it before King Rory O'Connor arrived.

King John visited Trim in 1210 to hold the de Lacy family in check. His visit gave the castle its alternative name, King John's Castle, but this is misleading as Walter de Lacy locked it up and left town, leaving the king to camp in a meadow outside. King John never actually stayed at Trim Castle.

When King John encountered Trim Castle and its locked gates it had begun to take on its present appearance as the first, largest and most formidable stone castle in Ireland. Walter de Lacy started the replacement of the wooden tower with a stone castle, but this transformation was not completed until 1224. De Lacy's grandson-in-law Geoffrey de Geneville oversaw the second stage in the castle's development. Geoffrey was a crusader who later became a Dominican monk at the abbey he himself founded nearby.

Today the green three-acre Trim Castle enclosure is dominated by a classic Norman keep which is 25m (82ft) high with square corner towers, and set on a motte.

Henry of Lancaster, later to become King Henry IV of England, was imprisoned in the Dublin Gate on the southern reach of the outer wall.

Trim was taken by Silken Thomas in 1536 and in 1647 by Catholic forces who opposed the English Parliamentarians. Trim was taken again by Cromwellian troops under Charles Coote in 1649, when the castle and town walls were badly damaged. The castle never recovered from this slighting.

Today the green three-acre castle enclosure is dominated by a classic Norman keep 25m (82ft) high and with square corner towers, set on a motte. Inside are three storeys, the lowest divided by a central wall. The main outer wall was built in around 1250, and it is an impressive fortification in its own right, 500 metres long and still more or less intact, in spite of the Parliamentarian onslaught. This curtain wall is interrupted by eight massive round towers and a gate-house. Within the north corner was a church. Facing the River Boyne which acts as a moat on one side was a Royal Mint, which produced 'Patricks' and 'Irelands' (Irish coins) into the fifteenth century. With its Norman keep and impressive curtain wall, Trim is reminiscent of Pevensey in Sussex.

Excavations in 1971 south of the keep uncovered the remains of ten headless men, who were probably criminals executed in the late middle ages. In 1465, Edward IV ordered that anyone who committed a robbery, or 'was going to rob', should be beheaded; their heads were mounted on spikes and publicly displayed as a warning to others.

MALAHIDE CASTLE

COUNTY DUBLIN

Malahide Castle is unique in remaining the property of one family, the Talbots, for over 790 years. The Talbot family became lords of Malahide in 1185 and occupied it until they sold it to the state in 1976, apart from an interlude in the mid-seventeenth century when Cromwell marched through Ireland. Cromwell took Malahide from the Catholic Royalist Talbots and granted the property to Miles Corbet. Corbet was one of the regicides who signed Charles I's death warrant and paid the price with his own life after the Restoration; then the Talbots got their castle back.

Malahide means, 'on the brow of the sea', and it stands on a low hill overlooking a bay north of Dublin. Its park has fine mature oaks and chestnuts dating to the sixteenth century. From the eighteenth century onwards the castle was developed as a great mansion.

The heart of the medieval castle is the Oak Room, which is approached by a winding stair and lit by Gothic windows added in 1820. The room is lined from floor to ceiling with carved oak panels showing scenes from scripture. It is likely that the Talbots covertly used this room as a family chapel at times when it was dangerous to be openly Catholic. Beside the Oak Room is the Great Hall, added in 1475. Unique in Ireland, the hall kept its original form and function, remaining a dining room until 1976. The huge painting of the Battle of the Boyne (1690) is a poignant reminder that on the morning of the historic battle 14 Talbot cousins, all of them followers of the Catholic James II, gathered to eat in the Great Hall at Malahide; not one of the 14 returned from the battle.

The early medieval castle was enlarged and embellished in the time of Edward IV. The west side of the castle had an early seventeenth century wing with four tapestried chambers. These were burnt in 1760 and replaced by two magnificent drawing rooms; the architect added round corner turrets to the exterior as a concession to the latest Gothic style. The facade was made incomparably grander in 1765 when two big flanking round towers were added.

Lord Talbot de Malahide died unexpectedly in 1973 while on a cruise. He was unmarried and left an unmarried sister to inherit the property together with crippling death duties. It was unfortunate that the Irish government refused to accept the castle and its contents in lieu of death duties, so the wonderful collection of furniture and portraits had to be sold at auction. Rose Talbot, the unlucky legatee, managed to pay the death duties and went to live in Tasmania. The Irish Tourist Board bought much of the furniture at auction and managed to reinstate it. The National Gallery purchased 35 of the family portraits and returned them to Malahide on loan. As a result of these rescue measures, the interior of Malahide Castle retains much of its original character and beauty.

A major feature of Malahide Castle Demesne is the beautiful Talbot Botanic Gardens. The gardens, as they exist today, were largely created by Lord Milo Talbot between 1948 and 1973. They cover an area of between 7 and 8 hectares (17 and 20 acres) of shrubbery and nearly 1.6 hectares (4 acres) of walled gardens.

BUNRATTY CASTLE

COUNTY CLARE

Bunratty (Bun Raite) Castle overlooks the River Shannon not far from Limerick. Its strategic position at the head of the Shannon estuary made it an inevitable focus for many a bloody battle. This in turn meant that it was repeatedly destroyed and rebuilt – no less than eight times. Surprisingly, in view of this history of multiple destructions, today Bunratty Castle is in excellent condition, and it is without question the finest surviving example of an Irish tower house.

After 1804 Bunratty Castle was allowed to fall into disrepair when the Studdart family abandoned it and built Bunratty House. The Castle was to return to its former splendour when Viscount Lord Gort purchased it in 1954. The extensive restoration work began in 1945 with the help of the Office of Public Works, the Irish Tourist Board and Shannon Development. It was then opened to the public in 1960 as a National Monument and is open to visitors year round. It is the most complete and authentically restored and furnished castle in Ireland.

Bunratty Castle had its beginnings more than a thousand years ago. In AD 950, the Vikings built a fortified trading post on this spot, which was once an island defended by a natural moat. When the Anglo-Normans arrived they recognized its strategic value and built the first stone structure on the site; Thomas de Clare built the first castle at Bunratty some time in the 1270s.

The very fine and impressive structure that we see today, with its high arch and two flanking square towers, dates from the fifteenth century, and it has walls 3m (10ft) thick that soar over five storeys high. It was the McNamara clan who built Bunratty, in 1425, but they did not hold onto it for very long. Subsequently Bunratty fell into the hands of the O'Briens, the Princes of Thomond, and they held it until the seventeenth century.

In the walls there are three murder holes. These enabled defenders to pour boiling water onto attackers below. The castle's centre-piece is its Great Hall, which is decorated with collections of medieval and Renaissance paintings, furniture and wall hangings: a major tourist attraction.

The Studdart family, an Anglo-Irish family, acquired Bunratty Castle in 1720. They lived in it until the nineteenth century. Then they abandoned it and built Bunratty House, which stands on a hill opposite the castle. In 1954 the castle was bought by the state and restored to its present splendid condition; it is now managed by the Shannon Development Company, which organizes twice-nightly four-course medieval Bunratty banquets complete with wine, medieval menus, court jesters and Irish harpists. The company also runs the adjacent Folk Park with its reconstructed traditional Irish village. The whole complex has been deliberately developed to make it into one of Ireland's top tourist attractions.

Bunratty Castle is a very simple and impressive building, a high and massive cube-shaped chunk of masonry resolving into big square towers at each corner, and with a battlemented roofline. In some ways it looks like a Norman keep, which historically was its point of origin. But the rather exotic battlements and the huge recessed central arch make it look something like the Gate of Ishtar in Babylon. Bunratty Castle is a very imposing and intriguing building and a deservedly popular tourist attraction.

CORCOMROE ABBEY

COUNTY CLARE

Corcomroe Abbey is picturesquely located in a green valley among the grey, windswept limestone hills of the Burren. The place is off the beaten track and visitors often find themselves alone in the abbey ruins. It nevertheless lies close to another monastic settlement, a cluster of three small early Christian churches nestling in the Pass of Oughmana and dedicated to St Colman.

Corcomroe Abbey was founded in about 1185 by King Donal Mor O'Brien as a Cistercian community. Corcomroe Abbey's nickname, Saint Mary of the Fertile Rock, tells us why the valley site was chosen; it was a place where a Cistercian community could support itself by growing its own food. The location set back a little from the coast was one often chosen for these communities. In the middle ages there were many pirate bands who systematically raided small coastal communities; some were slavers, and as late as the sixteenth and seventeenth centuries they were carrying off whole villages into slavery. Living just a few miles inland was much safer. Many medieval battles were fought in the area; there was great loss of life in one of these battles in 1267.

Most of the buildings have now gone, except the church, which is very well preserved though unroofed, and a few other stretches of wall around, all built of hard grey limestone. The church is cross-shaped with a chapel leading out of each transept, though one of these is now sealed off because it contains burials. Even so the groined entry arches are still visible, and the stone carving is of a high quality. The decorated pillar capitals carry the only Irish botanical carvings to be found from the twelfth century. Some more interesting carved images are to be seen in the transept chapels, which include masks with human faces and ingeniously carved dragons' heads. The choir has somehow kept its fine stone vault, which is criss-crossed by finely carved rib vaulting in Romanesque style. There is also a triple lancet window at the east end.

In the north wall of the choir there is a tomb-niche containing a remarkable effigy of King Conor na Siudaine O'Brien. This is a great rarity – one of the very few surviving images of a medieval Irish king. He wears a calf-length pleated gown and a spiked crown and carries a sceptre in his left hand. His feet rest on a cushion. King Conor, the grandson of the abbey's founder, looks exactly as a medieval king *should* look.

After the Dissolution of the monasteries in 1554, the abbey was passed to the Earl of Thomond, Murrough O'Brien, and then on to Donal O'Brien, who was the last native prince. It seems that monks were still formally attached to Corcomroe Abbey, as in 1628 a monk was appointed as abbot. Perhaps the remoteness of the area allowed old ways to continue unnoticed.

In the nineteenth century, the half-ruined church and its grounds were used as a graveyard, still a focal point for the local community.

CASHEL CASTLE

COUNTY TIPPERARY

The Rock of Cashel, or Rock of St Patrick, is a magnificent place, a great multiple ruin on a limestone hill at the edge of Cashel. Turning a bend in the main road between Dublin and Cork, the visitor is suddenly confronted by an extraordinary cluster of ancient buildings of different ages and purposes, like a miniature medieval city.

The fortress dates back to the fifth century AD and it has important links with early Christianity. This was Cashel, 'the stone fort', the seat of Irish kings and bishops through a period of 900 years. It was in its early days a royal fortress of the Eoghanacht clan, the rulers of the old Irish kingdom of Munster, for 400 years; their stronghold at Cashel witnessed the violent struggle by the Kings of Munster for power over the whole of Ireland.

In the 970s, the O'Neills of the north of Ireland were the dominant Irish clan. Things changed when Brian Boru was crowned King of Munster at Cashel in 977. He was probably crowned on the plinth of an ancient cross, the traditional crowning place of the Kings of Munster. Boru was a great warrior, and his prowess was such that in 997 the King of the O'Neills agreed on a division of Ireland with him. Brian Boru was not satisfied with half of Ireland and, when Dublin and Leinster revolted in 999, Boru put down their rebellion with such violence that the King of the O'Neills submitted to him in 1002.

In this way Brian Boru, working from his fortress at Cashel, succeeded in making himself High King of Ireland. During the next four years, Brian Boru undertook two tours of Ireland to show himself as High King of the whole island of Ireland. This technique of peregrination was very important, then and in later centuries; people needed to see their monarch, even if only occasionally, in order to feel any loyalty to him.

But Brian Boru's glory was short-lived. Leinster and Dublin rebelled again in 1013, provoking Boru to attack Leinster and lay siege to Dublin. He made the mistake of going home to celebrate Christmas. When he returned in 1014, the Vikings in Dublin had summoned extra troops from Scotland. The major battle that followed was the Battle of Clontarf, in which thousands died. Boru's army won, but Brian Boru himself was killed.

After that the O'Neill clan regained their dominant position. From having been the seat of the High King of Ireland, Cashel and Munster dwindled in significance. In the twelfth century, one of the high kings, Rory O'Connor of Connaught, conquered Munster before going on to attack Dublin.

Interwoven with this struggle for political power is another story, the ecclesiastical history of Cashel. Aenghus, King of Munster in the fifth century, was converted to Christianity by St Patrick. Following this conversion Patrick created a bishopric at Cashel. In 1101, the Rock of Cashel was granted to the Church and Bishop Cormac MacCarthy began work building a chapel. It still survives and is the most remarkable Romanesque church in the whole of Ireland. An impressive round tower was added. Perhaps the most imposing building on the Rock is the thirteenth century cathedral.

Altogether, the Rock of Cashel complex amounts to the most impressive collection of medieval buildings to be found anywhere in Ireland.

ROSS CASTLE

COUNTY KERRY

Ross Castle, which stands proudly on the shore of Killarney's Lower Lake, is one of the finest surviving examples of a medieval Irish chieftain's stronghold. The visible castle is thought to have been built in the middle of the fifteenth century by the O'Donaghue clan, though this structure may well replace an earlier stronghold.

Its most conspicuous feature is a tall, impressive and graceful stone tower or keep, which is something between a Norman keep and a Scottish tower house. It is a fine building in itself, with its corner tower and battlements. It was fitted with square bartizans, or corner turrets, which were built out from the upper walls at battlement level at opposite corners of the keep. The turrets enabled occupants to drop missiles on attackers below who might be attempting to undermine the tower corners, but perhaps more importantly gave them a full view of the exterior of each wall.

The castle's entrance door was unusual in an Irish castle. It was made of oak and was hinged on projecting stone brackets. The design allowed the defenders to defend the door from above.

The castle's great square tower stands in a square enclosure or bawn, which is surrounded by a fine battlemented curtain wall with round corner towers. Two of these towers are still standing. The other two were demolished in 1688 to make room for an extension, and the ruins of this can be seen on the south side of the castle.

Ross Castle was the seat and main stronghold of the O'Donaghue Mors, who were the hereditary rulers of the Killarney district; they were also the descendants of the ancient kings of Munster. After the Desmond rebellion their lands were acquired by the MacCarthy Mors, who sold them on to Sir Valentine Browne, the ancestor of the Earls of Kenmare. Legend has it that one of the O'Donaghues was sucked out of the window of the grand chamber at the top of the castle and disappeared into the lake with his horse, table and library. He supposedly lives on in a great palace at the bottom of the lake, keeping watch over subsequent events at the castle.

In 1652, Ross Castle was held by Lord Muskerry against a besieging Cromwellian army of 1,500 infantry and 700 cavalry commanded by Edmond Ludlow. Ross Castle finally fell to the Parliamentarian forces after floating batteries were brought in across the lough to bombard it. In 1690, the castle's owners were still the Browne family. They were Catholics and they had all their property confiscated for supporting the Jacobite cause. It was not until 1720 that the Brownes got their confiscated lands back. The castle itself remained in the hands of the government, who turned it into an army barracks.

The Brownes built themselves a new house a little to the north of the castle, and closer to the town. In time, as the military usefulness of the castle declined and it was abandoned, the castle turned into a kind of folly, in effect a very large-scale garden feature. Ross Castle Lodge now functions as a hotel.

BLARNEY CASTLE

COUNTY CORK

Blarney is one of those castle names that have strong resonances and associations that go beyond architecture, history or archaeology. It almost doesn't matter where it is. Like Balmoral, Harlech and Caernarvon, the name has a strong and characterful acquired meaning that transcends far beyond the geography and history of the place. 'Blarney' means something special – even to those who have never been there. Above all, it is thoroughly Irish.

Blarney Castle stands, with its village beside it, just 8km (5 miles) to the north-west of Cork. Blarney was originally created in the tenth century as a timber hunting lodge for the local chiefs, and a thousand years on it still stands in wooded country that has changed but little in all that time. The hunting lodge was rebuilt as a strong stone castle in 1210. The building that we see at Blarney today represents a third structure on the same site, a fifteenth century castle that was completed by the local chief Dermot McCarthy in 1446.

The castle remained the ancestral stronghold of the McCarthy family for exactly 200 years, withstanding several sieges until Oliver Cromwell and his cannon arrived to lay siege to it in 1646. Then the McCarthys were thrown out. Fifteen years later, after the restoration of Charles II, the McCarthys were given their castle back, and they took up residence there again.

After the Battle of the Boyne in 1690, all of the Irish chieftains were stripped of their powers, and many were evicted from their strongholds. The McCarthys were once more forced out of their castle, having regained it only a generation earlier. Blarney Castle was then largely demolished to make it indefensible before it was sold to Sir James Jeffryes, the Governor of Cork, in 1703.

The keep at Blarney Castle is a very powerful and impressive square building soaring 26m (85ft) into the air on stout walls 4m (13ft) thick. It looks even taller than this because it is perched picturesquely on a cliff edge. The massive keep is built five storeys high on an L-shaped plan. The lowest two levels are covered by a pointed stone vault. The slender tower that contains the main staircase and a few small chambers is evidently older than the main block. The keep is crowned with high, stepped battlements that jut out a full 60cm (23.5in) from the wall top; the overhang is supported by long inverted pyramid-shaped corbels, giving the castle a distinctive look and texture. This is crenellation on the grand scale, and it turns the keep into a very fine building.

The castle is best known for its Blarney Stone. This is a block of limestone a metre long, mounted high up on the wall of the keep, just below the battlements on the south side. To reach it, one has to climb one of the stone spiral staircases to the battlements. The stone is said to be one half of the Stone of Scone. This stone famously sat under the Coronation Chair in Westminster Abbey for several centuries, and has only recently been returned to Scotland, from where it was stolen by the English in the middle ages.

Blarney Castle is one of Ireland's oldest and most historic castles. It is famous for its stone - The Stone of Eloquence - which is traditionally believed to have the power to bestow the gift of eloquence on all those who kiss it.

Rock Close, on the grounds of Blarney Castle, is laid out on a pre-historic Druids site with the remains of huge boulders, rocks, a dolmen (a megalithic tomb with a large flat stone laid on uprights), a sacrificial altar and a witches' kitchen. You will find here Japanese bamboo trees, magnolias, Siberian dogwood and weeping willows and a stream which can be crossed via a small pedestrian bridge.

The Stone of Scone was an ancient crowning-stone, rather like the 'King's Stone' at Kingston-on-Thames. The Blarney Stone is said to have been given to Cormac McCarthy by King Robert the Bruce in 1314 in recognition of his support at the Battle of Bannockburn. On the other hand, the Stone of Scone originated in Ireland and was taken to Scotland in the dark ages, so it may after all be that the Blarney Stone represents a portion of the crowning stone that never left Ireland.

Probably it was a common practice in the dark ages for kings throughout the so-called Celtic lands to be installed while sitting or standing on a specially sanctified stone. At Tintagel Castle in Cornwall there is a carved footprint, which was probably used by Dumnonian kings during their dark age 'crowning' ceremonies. Probably we shall never know where the Blarney Stone came from, or why it was considered so special.

The strange connection between the stone and 'blarney' is explained by an episode in the sixteenth century. Elizabeth I wanted the chiefs of Ireland to agree to occupy their lands under title from her; she wanted them to acknowledge her overlordship. The Lord of Blarney, Cormac Teige McCarthy, was repeatedly asked for his submission to Elizabeth by George

Cardew, who was Elizabeth's Deputy in Ireland. Cormac handled each and every one of these requests with tact and subtle diplomacy, fulsomely promising his loyalty to the Queen, though carefully without conceding the issue of overlordship. Cardew duly reported this back to the Queen, who exploded, 'Blarney! What he says he never means. It's the usual Blarney!' After that the word Blarney became proverbial for 'the gift of the gab', empty promises or placation with smooth-talking deception; we still use it today, more than 400 years later.

Kissing the Blarney Stone is a slightly risky business, but it is said that those who risk it magically acquire Cormac Teige McCarthy's honey tongue. The stone is disinfected four times a day.

Today Blarney Castle forms part of an estate offering some pleasant woodland walks, the Blarney Castle Estate. Just 200m (656ft) south of the castle stands Blarney House, which was built in 1874. In the eighteenth century Sir John Jefferys built a Gothic Revival style house onto the castle, adding pointed windows and fanciful curving pinnacled battlements to his creation. Sad to say, this very picturesque house was burnt down in about 1820; only a semi-circular staircase from it still remains. Close by, the family built themselves a Scottish Baronial style house overlooking the lake – and also a megalithic garden folly. Clearly the tradition of good-natured eccentricity, the true spirit of Ireland, has been thoroughly maintained at Blarney Castle.

ST FIN BARRE'S CATHEDRAL

COUNTY CORK

St Fin Barre was the son of Amergin, chief smith to King Tighernach. Baptized with the name Luan, Fin Barre entered the priesthood and when he came to receive the tonsure, the monk who was cutting his hair commented, 'Fair is the hair of Luan.' Another monk said, 'Then let us call him Finn Barre.' 'Finn Barre' meant 'Fair Hair'.

St Fin Barre's Cathedral stands on a site that has been a place of worship since the seventh century. St Fin Barre founded a school there, and it was one of the five main monastic schools in Ireland from then until the tenth century. The only trace of the early monastic foundation that survives is the cemetery where the saint was buried.

There is little trace of the medieval monastic buildings either, though entries in the Chapter Minute Books give some clues as the size and appearance of the buildings in the middle ages. There are only a few blocks of carved stone from that period: a piscina, a square stone font, some carved heads, a carved doorway. The medieval cathedral has vanished because it was very severely damaged during the siege of Cork in 1689–90, when it came under heavy fire from the nearby Elizabethan fort. When the cathedral's steeple was demolished in 1865, shrapnel from the bombardment was found embedded in the masonry.

The foundation stone of a new building was laid in 1735 by Bishop Peter Browne. This was a small plain classical church, which incorporated the tower and spire of the medieval cathedral. In 1865 it was demolished because it was felt that the church was inadequate for the size of the diocese and did not have the dignity of a cathedral, though its fine entrance gate was left standing. The bells were removed to the Customs House Vaults and stored there during the demolition and rebuilding. They were hung in the new ringing room in 1870, and moved to the present bell chamber in 1903. The bells are inscribed with mottoes such as, *Fear God and Honour the King, Hark our Melody, May the Church Flourish and Her Enemies Decrease, May the Trade of This City Flourish, Let us Sound Praise to Our Benefactor, Come at My Call and Serve God All* and *Abel Rudhall of Gloucester in England Made Us All.*

William Burges became the architect of the new cathedral, winning a competition in which there were 63 entries. Burges was later criticized for sharp practice; he tendered below the stated maximum price of £15,000 by leaving out the cost of the towers, spires and carving. In the end, by the time it was completed in 1879, Burges's cathedral cost £100,000. Burges contributed, as his own gift to the cathedral, the golden Resurrection Angel. Burges drew up an iconographic scheme for the windows, maintained control over all the stages of the work, designed the sculptures, metalwork and furniture. The result is something unusual in a cathedral – a remarkable unity and consistency of style.

TIMOLEAGUE ABBEY

Timoleague Abbey stands on the edge of Timoleague village, which today is a colourful and prosperous little community living just a few steps from a sea inlet opening onto the Atlantic. The abbey had the benefit of being able to trade by sea, from which it gained some profit, though there were always risks in being a coastal community.

The abbey was built on the site of St Molga's Well. Like many another saint's well, this was probably a pagan cult focus before it was adopted and converted by Christians. Rivers, streams, pools, springs and wells were venerated in the pre-Christian period, and ancient ceremonies like well-dressing have continued to the present day. On Ascension Day at Rorrington on the Wales-Shropshire border, locals used to meet at the hillside well, which was decorated with 'a bower of green boughs, rushes and flowers' and a Maypole was raised. Then people 'used to walk round the hill with fife, drum and fiddle, dancing and frolicking as they went.' Around 1200 of these holy wells are known to have existed, and certainly many more have been lost – abandoned, overgrown and forgotten. One of the finest Christian chapels to be built over a converted sacred spring is the one at Holywell in Clwyd. Probably the well at Timoleague was of the same type, only it had an abbey built over it.

Timoleague Abbey was founded in 1240 by MacCarthy Reach, Lord Carbery, and extended in 1312 by Donal Glas McCarthy. The buildings on the site date from various periods, and the abbey was extended again in the early sixteenth century, by Irish patrons, shortly before the Dissolution. Certainly the current church, a roofless ruin but with its tower intact, is not the first to stand on the site. The original church was shorter. It was probably lengthened when the portion including the tower was added by Edmund de Courcy, Bishop of Ross, late in the fifteenth century.

In 1642, Timoleague Abbey was sacked by English soldiers under Lord Forbes, who smashed all the stained glass windows before burning the place down. Even so, a lot of the original stonework has survived. The church, the infirmary, the refectory and a walled courtyard are all still standing. There are also cloisters and a wine cellar. The architecture of Timoleague was very plain indeed by comparison with Corcomroe Abbey, for instance, and must have been very austere even when complete. But the friars who lived there did not live austere lives. They had a penchant for the finer things in life, and were financially prosperous thanks to their trade with Spanish wine merchants.

As at other religious houses in Ireland, Timoleague survived the Reformation, for a time. The friars were able to remain at the abbey until 1629. Brother Michael O'Cleary visited Timoleague at about that time to copy manuscripts for his compilation of texts, *The Annals of the Four Masters*.

Today, Timoleague Abbey is a rather bleak and unromantic roofless ruin, but it still acts as a graveyard for the local people.

Timoleague Abbey stands picturesquely at the water's edge at the head of a long sea inlet. In its day it was one of the largest and most important of the religious houses in Ireland.

DUNROBIN CASTLE

Dunrobin Castle is a cross between a French château and a fairytale palace – or a creation of Walt Disney – and altogether the unlikeliest building to stumble upon in the Scottish Highlands. It stands north of Dornoch Firth, between Golspie and Brora, on the edge of a sea-cliff that could once have given the castle a wildly romantic air, but has instead been tamed and manicured into an elegant flight of terraces and gardens. And the unexpectedness of the place does not end there. The grounds are green and luxuriant, while the moors not far away inland are barren and brown.

Dunrobin is a fascinating place, not quite real, a sort of secret garden in the Highlands. In spite of having the impeccably well-groomed appearance of a great mansion, it is in fact a real castle and a very ancient one. The Scottish kings who took Sutherland back from the Norsemen in the twelfth century granted it to Hugh de Moravia; Hugh's son William was created Earl of Sutherland in 1235. Dunrobin is mentioned in documents as being the stronghold of the Earls of Sutherland in 1401, but the ancient tower that survives, all but hidden, at the very heart of the building may well be older than that.

The Earldom of Sutherland is the oldest in Scotland and by ancient tradition if there are no male heirs the earldom may pass through the female line. When this actually happened in the sixteenth century it led to a fierce and bloody dispute. When it happened again in the seventeenth century the result was more peaceable but it still led to a long and costly legal dispute. The Sutherland estate is a very substantial piece of property indeed – and one that is well worth fighting for. The law eventually decided in favour of Elizabeth, whose father, the eighteenth Earl, had died when she was one year old. She became nineteenth Countess and married an Englishman, George Leveson-Gower, who was shortly afterwards to become Marquess of Stafford; shortly before his death he was created Duke of Sutherland. This is a rare example of a man enhancing his social status by marriage – but then everything about Dunrobin is rare and out of the ordinary.

The marriage of Elizabeth and George led to the creation of one of the wealthiest and most brilliant families in nineteenth century Britain. When her husband was English ambassador to France, the 'Countess-Duchess' lent her clothes to Marie-Antoinette for the desperate escape attempt that she and her family made; they were stopped, recognized and arrested at Varennes. The first Duke inherited the Duke of Bridgewater's fortune in addition to his own; he was described as a 'Leviathan of Wealth'. An enormous statue of him stands on a mountainside near Golspie. But he was a callous landowner, lacking in common humanity. To make himself even richer, he was responsible for ordering the Highland Clearances. Many crofters were forcibly and cruelly turned off their land. While some like to blame the factors and other employees who carried out the Duke's orders to evict, the Duke must be held responsible for giving the orders.

The formal gardens were laid out in 1850 by Barry, the architect who built the Victorian extension to Dunrobin and also the Houses of Parliament in London.

The third Duke of Sutherland, who owned 5,260,913 hectares (1,300,000 acres), was to become the biggest landowner in Western Europe.

Most of the exterior of the castle was built by the second Duke, who commissioned Sir Charles Barry to design additions to the eighteenth century house in French Renaissance style, complete with picturesque dormer windows and high pointed conical tower roofs. Work began in 1834 to Barry's design, with slight modifications by the building contractor, W. Leslie of Aberdeen. Barry visited Dunrobin in 1848, and designed the imposing entrance tower.

Caen stone, imported all the way from France, was used for the staircase. This is architecturally the finest part of the castle's interior; much of Dunrobin was gutted when fire broke out in 1915 while the castle was being used as a naval hospital. When the First World War was over, the burnt-out rooms were redesigned by Sir Robert Lorimer, and repaired and redecorated. Lorimer created a panelled Dining Room, where five big family portraits hang. There is a painting of the second Duchess, Harriet, by Winterhalter; she was Mistress of the Robes and a close friend of Queen Victoria, who

This beautiful castle with a French influence sits looking out across the North Sea and is well worth a visit. The 189 rooms contain many collections of furniture, pictures, objets d'art, uniforms, china and family memorabilia. There is also a nineteenth century horsedrawn fire engine in the Sub Hall and a museum which is housed in the old summer house.

stayed at Dunrobin Castle more than once.

Lorimer created the long Drawing Room out of two earlier rooms. Here two magnificent paintings by Canaletto are on display, along with some fine French furniture. There is a vaulted corridor, from which there is a view of the castle's ancient tower and courtyard.

In the gardens below the terraces there is a castle museum. This was once a banqueting house, but during the course of the nineteenth century it filled up with a collection of curiosities, including 400 animal heads, as well as other oddments such as weapons, coins, Lord Raglan's cap, Garibaldi's slippers and Queen Victoria's handkerchief. The collection also includes the skulls of the sons of King Lochlin of Denmark. It is not a museum in any modern sense, but a fine example of an eighteenth or nineteenth century 'cabinet of curiosities', and therefore a museum piece in itself.

Dunrobin Castle is a delightful creation and the family that created it is full of interest, but it is an extremely uncomfortable thought for many of us that this huge display of wealth was built on the misery of the first Duke of Sutherland's tenants; already extremely poor, many of them were dispossessed, and often brutally, in the interests of further profit for their callous landlord.

EILEAN DONAN CASTLE

ROSS-SHIRE

Eilean Donan is the ultimate picturesque Highland castle, perched on a little rocky island in a loch. It has its roots deeply implanted in remote antiquity. The name itself means 'Island of Donan', a hermit who lived there in the seventh century. Donan moved to a monastic foundation on the island of Eigg, where in 618 he was set upon by marauders and beheaded along with 52 of his companions.

Opposite the castle is a human footprint carved in the living rock. This tells us that the place was a royal centre in the dark ages and possibly much earlier. There is a similar footprint at Tintagel in Cornwall, which was probably used for oath-taking ceremonies such as coronations.

The castle that we now see dates from the late thirteenth century. Only archaeological investigation can determine whether the remains of Viking-period defences lie underneath the stone keep and its outer enclosing wall. In 1263 a vast Viking fleet made its way south along the west coast of Scotland, past Eilean Donan, to engage Alexander III of Scotland at Largs. The invaders were resoundingly defeated and limped back to Norway. This event marked the end of 400 years of Scandinavian control. By the Treaty of Perth of 1266, the Highlands and Islands passed to the Scottish Crown.

By the end of the thirteenth century Eilean Donan had passed into the hands of Kenneth Mackenzie, in spite of repeated attempts by the Earl of Ross to take it from him.

Tradition has it that John Mackenzie sheltered Robert the Bruce at Eilean Donan when he was out of favour with many of the clan chiefs and being hunted by the English. By 1331, Robert's fortunes had changed; he had defeated his enemies and established himself as King of Scotland.

The dispute over the ownership of the castle between the Mackenzies and the Earls of Ross continued. The Earl threatened to take it by force, but a royal charter of 1362 (from King David II) confirmed the Mackenzies' title, and they managed to hold the castle for the next two centuries. The MacRaes had settled in the district and they became known as the Mackenzies' 'Coat of Mail', their bodyguard. But the Earldom of Ross had not given up. When Euphemia Countess of Ross was widowed for the second time in 1427, she cast about for a third husband, and her eye fell on the young Alexander Mackenzie (and his castle). He turned her down and she promptly had him thrown in prison. The Constable of Eilean Donan retaliated by taking one of her kinsmen as a hostage to exchange for the young Mackenzie. The Countess agreed the exchange and Alexander Mackenzie was released.

Although the island of Eilean Donan has been a fortified site for at least 800 years, the present building largely dates from the early twentieth century. Today's castle was re-built between 1912 and 1932 by Lieutenant Colonel John MacRae-Gilstrap.

In the late fifteenth century the castle shrank. The old enclosure wall was dismantled and new defences were raised enclosing a smaller precinct. The MacRaes became constables of the castle in 1509 and took control of the whole district. The Lordship of the Isles had been extinguished as a political force, but in 1530 Donald Gorm MacDonald of Sleat foolishly tried to revive it for himself. Nine years later, Donald sailed to Applecross with 50 galleys to lay waste the Mackenzie lands before heading for Eilean Donan, which was rumoured to be lightly garrisoned.

The castle was indeed lightly garrisoned: it was held by only three men, the constable John Matheson, the young Duncan MacRae and a watchman. They bravely shut the gate against Donald's soldiers, who resorted to firing arrows at the windows. One of these hit Matheson, leaving only the watchman and Duncan McRae. They ran short of ammunition. Duncan was left with only one barbed arrow, which he kept by him until he could use it to good effect. Donald used a battering ram to force the gate; then Duncan shot him in the foot. Donald impatiently pulled the arrow out and in doing so severed one of his own arteries. The bleeding was so intense that the MacDonalds withdrew in haste, putting the injured Donald MacDonald into a boat and landing him near Avernish at a place called Larachtaigh Mhic-Dhomhnuill, 'the site of MacDonald's house'. There he bled to death. It was an historic moment, marking the end of the Lordship of the Isles.

Gunpowder changed everything. It may be that the hornwork added to the south-east angle of the castle in the fifteenth century was created to accommodate new guns.

Three years after the failure of the 1715 Stuart rebellion, a plot was hatched to try to land a large force of Spaniards in England and a smaller force of Spaniards and Jacobites in Scotland, and there meet the Highland contingent. The 'armada' sailing to England was badly crippled but the smaller contingent reached Scotland, landing close to Eilean Donan. A force under General Wightman set out from Inverness to intercept the Jacobite force. In May 1719 three naval vessels under Captain Boyle sailed into Kintail and laid siege to Eilean Donan, capturing it after a short bombardment. Troops from the ships entered the castle and used its own ammunition stores to blow it up, at least to the extent of rendering it unusable. Another version of events is also told, which has the defenders of the castle, Colonel Donald Murchison and Christopher MacRae, deliberately sabotaging the castle to prevent it from falling into Government hands.

The ruins were neglected for 200 years until 1912, when Lt-Col John MacRae-Gilstrap bought it and began restoration work. He was helped by Farquhar MacRae who had had a dream telling him exactly what the original structure had looked like; this was later confirmed by plans held in Edinburgh Castle. The beautifully rebuilt castle was finished in 1932, together with a bridge to the mainland, and is now open to the public. The kitchen and bedrooms can be seen, as well as the barrel-vaulted Billeting Room for off-duty soldiers. There is a very fine Banqueting Hall in romantic baronial style, containing a display of Jacobite memorabilia – including a lock of Bonnie Prince Charlie's hair.

BALMORAL CASTLE

Following a holiday visit to Scotland which she greatly enjoyed in 1842, Queen Victoria decided to take out a lease on the small Deeside castle of Balmoral as a holiday home. Rather surprisingly, she took the little castle on without having set eyes on it. She saw it for the first time six years later and was very pleased with it. She described it as 'a pretty little castle in the old Scottish style' and 'the finest I have seen anywhere', which were odd comments in view of what was to happen next.

The castle Victoria stayed in initially was an early nineteenth century mansion, which had been raised after the Earl of Fife had bought the estate in 1798. This mansion which Victoria so admired was designed by an Aberdeen architect by the name of John Smith. Before that, the Balmoral estate had been the property of Sir Robert Gordon and his descendants. Before that it had belonged to the Farquharsons of Inverey. An even earlier castle had stood on the site, a small Scottish stone tower house that was built in about 1390 by Sir William Drummond, though it seems not to have been mentioned in any records until 1484.

But the chequered history of Balmoral Castle was not over with the arrival of Queen Victoria in 1848. She had a large family and she and Prince Albert soon found the attractive little mansion 'too small' for their needs. Prince Albert bought the freehold of Balmoral from the trustees of Sir Robert Gordon as a present for Victoria in 1852, at a cost of £31,000. It came with a substantial shooting and fishing estate amounting to 4,451.5 hectares (11,000 acres).

Now that they owned it, the Queen and Prince Albert could do as they liked with it. They had the house knocked down and a completely new, and of course bigger, house built 100m (328ft) away. The site of the old house is marked by a stone. Prince Albert had a major role in designing the new house, which was in the fashionable neo-Gothic Scottish Baronial style, complete with gables, towers, turrets and crenellations. It has to be said that the proportions of Albert's Balmoral leave a lot to be desired. The Great Tower, which stands massively to attention at one end is top-heavy with bartizans – too massive and just far too big for the rest of the house. It is joined to the rest of the house by what seems in comparison a grotesquely low range. The main block is, in itself, very well designed, picturesque and well-proportioned; it would look far better without its Great Tower looming 30m (98ft) high beside it, even though there are some fine views from the top. The main facade is imposing and built in the local grey

granite, which makes an excellent building stone.

Memorial cairns to various members of the Royal Family have been raised on a nearby mountain, Craig Gowan. The new and thoroughly Victorian Balmoral Castle, the Balmoral we see today, was completed in 1855. It remained one of Queen Victoria's favourite houses for the rest of her life and she went on staying there after Prince Albert's death. She loved Balmoral and she loved Scotland too, describing it as 'the proudest, finest country in the world.' When she became a reclusive widow, she divided her time between Balmoral and Osborne, which Albert had also helped to design. Victoria wrote adoringly of both Balmoral and her husband, 'My dearest Albert's own creation, own work, own building, own laying out.'

Prince Albert laid out the gardens and grounds near the house. The Duke of Edinburgh, the consort of the present Queen, continued this tradition by recently enlarging the flower and vegetable garden and creating a water garden. It was not just Queen Victoria who loved Balmoral. Successive kings and queens since Victoria have also loved the place – not least because of the sense of freedom and privacy it gives, so precious to those who live their lives constantly in the public eye. The castle is perched up at around 250m (820ft) above sea level, 'away from it all'. It is possible, even in these times of unscrupulous press intrusion, for the Royal Family to walk, fish, shoot and picnic on the estate at Balmoral without any thought of being watched. It is not surprising that the present Queen enjoys her annual family holiday at Balmoral each August.

The estate is now five times larger than when Queen Victoria acquired it, and it employs about 50 full-time and 100 part-time staff. The estate is privately owned and funded by the Queen. Among the attractions to the Royal Family are the possibilities it offers for salmon fishing, grouse shooting and hill walking.

Balmoral is a castle by name, but really a country house by function. Interestingly its name is Gaelic for 'majestic dwelling', which just about sums it up. Balmoral stands 12km (7.5 miles) west of Ballater and only about 2km (1.2 miles) from Crathie church, which the Queen uses when she is in residence. Crathie church was built in 1903, and replaced the old kirk built a hundred years earlier. Another 2km (1.2 miles) to the west stands Abergeldie Castle. This is another Highland royal residence, which is an ancient building that has been added to in modern times to make it more comfortable. Abergeldie Castle was used by Edward VII when Prince of Wales, while his mother stayed at Balmoral; after her death and his accession to the throne, Abergeldie became a shooting lodge.

The estate grounds, gardens and exhibitions at Balmoral are open to the public every day from the middle of April until the last day of July, so long as the Royal Family is not in residence. Usually the Queen arrives for her holiday there in August, and then the estate is closed to visitors. There are several cottages on the estate which can be rented as holiday homes.

Balmoral Castle has remained a favourite residence for The Queen and her family during the summer. The Castle is located on the large Balmoral Estate, a working estate which aims to protect the environment while contributing to the local economy.

CRAIGIEVAR CASTLE

ABERDEENSHIRE

Craigievar is one of those castles that is too good to be true. It is like a castle out of a fairy-tale, taller than it is wide, with soaring walls and a roofline that bristles with gables, chimneys, corbelled round corner turrets and conical spires. A flag flies from one of the spires; really there should be pennants flying from all of them. There should be a damsel with long tresses leaning wistfully out of at least one of the many turret windows. Craigievar's setting too is straight out of a fairy tale. It stands just to the south of the village of Muir of Fowlis near Alford in a beautifully landscaped park, surrounded by trees, shrubs and sloping lawns.

The reality is that Craigievar Castle is of no great antiquity. It was built in 1626 by William Forbes as a tower house. William Forbes was a merchant from Aberdeen, who had made a fortune trading with ports in the Baltic. He used his wealth to build his own tower house. Like many another Scottish tower house it was built on an L-shaped ground plan. It rises six storeys high above smooth, unscalable walls. The castle was built to standard Scottish fortress specifications, with small and rather few windows puncturing the lower walls, very heavy doors and an iron yett (a gate in the form of a heavy grille). It also had a surrounding curtain wall with a squat round tower at each corner, though unfortunately only one of these has survived. It stands beside the castle, looking like a rather fancy summer house.

In spite of these seriously expensive design features, it seems that Craigievar Castle was to serve primarily as a stately home rather than as a real fortress. In fact, by the time it was built in the 1620s, the age of the castle-fortress was over. Weapons technology had developed to a point where masonry could not withstand an attack by cannon, so the centuries-old concept of the castle as a stronghold was becoming obsolete. The tower house nevertheless continued to be a good defence against casual raiders, robbers and bandits; it was certainly burglar-proof. Perhaps more importantly, the castle architecture had become associated with high status, so high-status families continued to want castles.

Craigievar Castle's interior was luxuriously appointed. Many of the rooms have survived remarkably unchanged from the seventeenth century. There are some fine Jacobean vaulted and plastered ceilings, and there is Jacobean panelling to match. The period charm of Craigievar Castle made it an early attraction for tourists, and its reputation was greatly enhanced by a visit from Queen Victoria and Prince Albert, together with many of the crowned heads of Europe who were their guests.

This castle was never abandoned, like Kilchurn, but remained in occupation by its owners, William Forbes and his descendants, for most of its history. It was only in 1963 that it was passed, along with 120 hectares (296.5 acres) of land, into the hands of the National Trust for Scotland.

CRATHES CASTLE

ABERDEENSHIRE

Crathes Castle stands close to the A93, 5km (3 miles) east of Banchory and 20km (12.5 miles) south-west of Aberdeen. Crathes Castle is an impressive L-plan tower house, built with four storeys and an attic. It was founded by the Burnett family in the sixteenth century. Alexander Burnett of Leys began work on it in 1553, and it took 46 years to complete. The massive tower tapers towards the top. This gives the structure greater stability and also makes it much easier to drop missiles onto attackers who might attempt to scale the walls. The weak point of the classic Norman square keep was its corners; it was possible to loosen stones from the corners, and so destabilize the entire structure. At Crathes, the corners were rounded, to make this much harder to do.

The entrance was fitted with an iron yett. On the turnpike stair, a tripping stone was installed. This was one step set at a different height from all the rest. The residents, defending the castle, would soon become familiar with this odd step and not be bothered by it, but a newcomer to the building, an intruder, would be likely to stumble on it when attempting to run up the stairs. Then it would be up to the defenders to take advantage of the fall, which could delay the invasion of the building by several valuable seconds.

The lower storeys were originally built with minimal window openings and smooth walls for defensive reasons. The upper storeys, well out of reach from ground attack were fitted with larger windows and a variety of corbelled juts and turrets. A rather incongruous two-storey range was a later addition built on in the eighteenth century. No attempt was made to match the style or scale of the original; the castle would look better without it. A late Victorian wing tacked on by the eleventh Baronet in the late nineteenth century was destroyed by fire in 1966 and not rebuilt.

Crathes is extremely well preserved. Its interior is embellished with portraits, oak ceilings, heraldic shields and Jacobean painted ceilings that were only uncovered in 1877. Also on display is a jewelled ivory horn, which is thought to have been given to the Burnetts by Robert the Bruce when he granted them the Lands of Leys in 1323.

In 1951 Sir James Burnett of Leys handed over Crathes Castle and 87 hectares (215 acres) of land to the National Trust of Scotland together with an upkeep endowment. The castle is open daily April–October and the surrounding gardens and woodland are open all the year round.

SLAINS CASTLE

ABERDEENSHIRE

The broken shell of Old Slains Castle stands on the windswept sea-cliffs between Aberdeen and Peterhead. This was a seat of the Hay family, the Earls of Erroll. The lands belonging to Slains were given to Sir Gilbert Hay by Robert the Bruce as a reward for his services in the armed struggle against the English. Sir Gilbert was also appointed High Constable of Scotland.

Sir Gilbert was succeeded by his son Sir David, who went with David II to the Battle of Neville's Cross in 1346; the King was captured and Sir David was killed. William Hay was created Earl of Erroll and Lord of Slains by James II as a reward for his support in the King's war against the 'Black' Douglas lords and their allies the Lyndsays and the MacDonalds. The rebel lords were eventually defeated by the Gordons and the 'Red' Douglas. The Hays were allies of the Gordons.

The tower of Old Slains dates from around this time. It was an oblong keep five storeys high, with a vaulted basement entered at courtyard level. The second storey was entered, English-style, by an external staircase, in this case a collapsible wooden staircase, a little like some old iron fire escapes. The battlements were probably fitted with bartizans, or open, roofless turrets, at each corner. There was a pitched roof with chimneys on top. There was also an overhanging box machicolation positioned directly above the staircase entrance. This was installed not just to bomb attackers trying to force open the door, but to ensure the destruction of the staircase itself in time of siege. Inside the tower there was a stone spiral staircase that connected all the different levels from the second storey upwards.

To begin with, in the fifteenth century, the tower was surrounded by a wooden palisade. Beyond that it was protected on three sides by the cliffs and on the fourth side by a ditch. In the early sixteenth century the palisade was replaced by a stone curtain wall with a stone-built gatehouse. Anti-personnel cannon were installed. On the landward side of the ditch was a 'castle town' village, the sort of settlement that flourished beside such towers. This consisted of a cluster of wattle buildings with thatched roofs, consisting of stables, barns and workshops. This village was probably also defended by an outer ditch.

At the Battle of Sauchieburn in 1488 William Hay, third Earl of Erroll, and other supporters abandoned James III of Scotland to his fate. The Hays switched their support to the new king, James IV. In 1513, the Hays (87 gentlemen all bearing the same surname) were all killed at the Battle of Flodden along with James IV.

The huge ruin of Slains Castle stands on the cliffs above the sea. It incorporates part of the basement of the sixteenth century tower house of Bowness. The castle now consists of buildings around a central courtyard with adjoining ranges.

Slains Castle today is a slightly unsettling place. It comes as little surprise to discover that Bram Stoker, who stayed at the castle, used it as inspiration for his story of Dracula. Earlier distinguished visitors included Johnson and Boswell who stayed here in 1773 and noted that 'the walls of one of the towers seemed only to be a continuation of the perpendicular rock the foot of which is beaten by the waves'.

In 1594, both Old Slains Castle and the Hay residence of Delgatie Castle were destroyed under James VI's personal supervision, as a punishment for the Hays' involvement in a Catholic Spanish plot. Not long before, the Hays had been suspected of complicity in the Spanish Armada. James VI was furious at these entanglements, as they endangered his chances of achieving the English throne. Francis Hay, the ninth Earl of Erroll, wisely fled the country. When he returned three years later, he decided to rebuild Bowness Castle to the north of Old Slains – and named it New Slains.

New Slains also stands commandingly on the sea-cliffs. The twentieth Earl of Erroll was forced by death duties to sell the castle in 1916. Unfortunately the new owner did not maintain it and it was finally unroofed for safety reasons in 1925, turning it instantly into a modern ruin. Bram Stoker had Slains in mind for the vampire's home when he wrote *Dracula*; Stoker often stayed in Cruden Bay nearby.

During the Armada fiasco, in which the Hays were involved as conspirators, many Spanish ships were wrecked along the coastline of Scotland and Ireland. Some of the wrecks were caused by attempts to moor close inshore in order to warn Scottish and Irish lords friendly to the Catholic cause not to invade England, because it was not safe to do so; the Duke of Parma's troops, an invasion army 20,000 strong, had failed to reach England.

One galleon was wrecked off Tantallon Castle while their masters were trying to make contact with the 'Red' Douglas, and another near St Andrews Castle, though it is not known who the Spanish were trying to contact there. Another was wrecked off Old Slains Castle while trying to warn the Hays. The Old Slains garrison must have had a clear view of this galleon as it foundered nearby. Whether the Hays sent any boats out to save the drowning sailors is not recorded, but it is unlikely that they could have done anything as the storm that blew up was sudden and severe. All three vessels were wrecked at the same time. Curiously, the 'Red' Douglas, Archibald the eighth Earl of Angus, died on the same night.

The fact that the Hays of Erroll and the Gordons of Huntly were ready to come out in open rebellion against King James VI implies that they expected strong support from elsewhere. They perhaps had reason to suppose that the Spanish were about to intervene; in fact they may have been party to a conspiracy of the same type as the Spanish Armada, where an invasion was planned to coincide with a rebellion. But no Spanish ships appeared and the Hays and the Gordons lost their castles in the gamble. In fact it was not until three years later, in 1597, that the Armada was ready to sail. This time 84 mostly new galleons were assembled in Galicia. But the Hays had lost Old Slains and there was no possibility of their having anything further to do with a Spanish invasion. The Spanish had proved so unreliable and so incompetent that they could no longer rely on any help from within Britain, and because of that there could be no invasion.

BRAEMAR CASTLE

ABERDEENSHIRE

John Erskine, Earl of Mar, who was High Treasurer of Scotland and guardian of James VI (James I of England), built his castle at Braemar in 1628. It was a strategically sensitive position, where the road from the pass to the south descends into the upper Dee valley. The castle is well situated, on a little knoll looking out commandingly across the Dee valley.

The Earl's neighbours, the Farquharson clan, had for a very long time been enemies of the Erskines. Sixty years after Braemar was built Grahame of Claverhouse, known as 'Bonnie Dundee', raised the Stuart standard. The Earl of Mar made no move to join him and John Farquharson, a fiery Jacobite known as 'The Black Colonel', used this as an excuse to set fire to Braemar Castle to prevent it falling into the hands of government forces. Braemar was in ruins for over 50 years.

In the Jacobite rising of 1715, another Earl of Mar had supported the Stuarts, and as a punishment for this he had his Deeside estates confiscated. In 1732 the burnt-out shell of Braemar Castle was sold to the Farquharson family who had destroyed it, and they leased it for £14 a year to the government. Following the 1745 rebellion, the government set about establishing strong points round the Highlands to prevent any further rebellion. They restored Braemar Castle and installed a garrison. In 1807, the garrison left and the Farquharsons regained possession. They were able to entertain Queen Victoria there when she attended the Braemar games.

Braemar Castle is built as a conventional L-plan tower house, five storeys tall, with a large newel staircase built in the angle to give easy access to rooms in both wings on each level. Often the corner turrets, or bartizans, on tower houses are quaint and picturesque, but Braemar's rather functional cylindrical turrets are too tall and too bulky. Aesthetically the effect is heavy and clumsy. The overall design of the castle is of great architectural interest, though, because it shows very well the style of the later tower houses, with their emphasis on residential comfort and convenience.

When the Hanoverian government leased the castle in 1748, the architect charged with restoring it was John Adam. He heightened the staircase tower and bartizans, replacing their conical tiled roofs with flat battlemented tops that were more practical in terms of eighteenth century warfare. Adam also added a curtain wall round the castle, with six sharp-angled projections provided with gun-slits that were designed to cover the approaches to the castle. This may have done its job in purely practical terms, but aesthetically the wall is too low in relation to the scale of the tower house; the structure as a whole would look better if the curtain wall was two or three times taller. Probably there was an earlier curtain wall creating a protective enclosure round the main building.

The exterior is rather bleak, but the scale of the interior is cozy and intimate; it is a castle that would be pleasant to live in, offering attractive views across meadows to the River Dee.

FYVIE CASTLE

ABERDEENSHIRE

Fyvie Castle, 35km (22 miles) north-west of Aberdeen, is the finest example there is of Scottish baronial architecture. Many ancient buildings – castles, churches and cathedrals especially – bear witness to the various times in which they were developed, each addition and each building phase representing the tastes and preoccupations of a particular generation. Nowhere is this more true than at Fyvie, yet with a surprising outcome.

The castle has five towers, each one built by and named after one of the five families who owned Fyvie in succession. On the south side, the Meldrum Tower stands on the left, the Preston Tower on the right. In the centre the Seton Tower forms a grand arched entrance; this tall, spectacular and highly original gatehouse was the work of Alexander Seton, the Earl of Dunfermline, in 1599. It is already a nostalgic backward glance at the age of chivalry, with its carved dormer windows, armorial panels and fantastic corbelled turrets. The Gordon Tower was added in 1777 and the Leith Tower was built in 1899. The Leith Tower was modelled on Huntly Castle and it incorporates music and billiard rooms, a gallery and an organ. This may sound like a hotch-potch of add-ons and extensions, but the overall effect is extremely harmonious; in spite of the way it developed, Fyvie has turned out to be an orderly, symmetrical and very beautiful building.

The castle is three lofty storeys high but mostly only one room deep, with the rooms opening into one another, rather like the long sequence of rooms at Petworth. The great set-piece of the castle interior is the elaborate processional staircase, which was built by Seton in 1605. Strongly influenced by contemporary French architecture, it is lavishly decorated with heraldry. The Morning Room has amazing seventeenth century plasterwork. There is also a spectacular collection of pictures, including paintings by Raeburn, Romney, Gainsborough and Hoppner.

Undoubtedly one of the finest castles in Scotland, Fyvie can trace its royal connections back to 1211 and William the Lion.

The first significant documented record of Fyvie is in 1296, when Edward I visited. A little later, the castle became one of Robert the Bruce's royal residences; he set aside a tract of the adjoining countryside as a royal hunting forest. In 1397 Fyvie Castle passed into the hands of the Preston family; it was Sir Henry Preston, who fought at the Battle of Otterburn, who built one of the towers. In 1596, Fyvie was bought from the Meldrums by Alexander Seton, another of the tower-builders. Seton went on to achieve a peerage, and attended Parliament as the first Lord Fyvie.

The castles and its estate were seized by the Crown in 1689, following the death of the third Lord Fyvie; he made the mistake of fighting on the wrong side at the Battle of Killiecrankie. In the 1740s, Fyvie passed into the hands of the Gordons. This was the family that produced Lord Byron, and the traditional dance, the Gay Gordons.

Surrounded by extensive grounds, including an original walled kitchen garden, a restored ice-house and landscaped woodlands, Fyvie is open to the public during the summer months. Fyvie Castle is unquestionably one of the finest mansions in Scotland.

CLAYPOTTS CASTLE

ANGUS

After the sixteenth century Reformation in Scotland, when the age of castles was all but over, more modest fortified houses were built by and for lairds who owned just one modest estate. The home of the Strachan family near Dundee is a typical example of these post-Reformation tower houses. At Claypotts it is easy to see how these structures got their name. Claypotts really is a house hoisted up on top of a tower.

Even before the Reformation, the Strachans were lay tenants of land belonging to three abbeys. For their main holding, which was Claypotts, they paid an annual rent of £12 and twelve cockerels. After the Reformation, the Strachans' hold on the land was strengthened and John Strachan embarked on a new building that would reflect his new status. As we see again and again, castle-building was frequently a display of social status and power.

The structure, which has the date 1569 carved on it, was built on what is sometimes described as a Z-plan, with two massive round towers projecting from opposite corners of the main block. Twelve wide-mouthed gunholes puncture the walls down at ground level, which are obviously there to enable the Strachans to shoot down marauders. These and other features, such as the iron grilles over the windows and the wooden drawbars behind the window shutters and doors are really equivalents of today's security lights and door-chains. They are not so much military as domestic; the Strachans were really only keeping out burglars.

Claypotts, which is extremely well preserved, was similar to earlier tower houses, only with some refinements. Two staircases were provided, one for the gentlefolk, and one for the servants. The sanitation was improved; the draughty latrines were replaced by portable soil boxes, rather like chemical toilets, which could be emptied as required.

The tower house that we see at Claypotts was built right at the end of the castle tradition; it had become refined into a comfortable but fairly compact lord's residence. John Strachan's will, made in the 1590s, shows that he was not by any means rich, but he was a cut above the average farmer.

Claypotts was an influential castle. When King James VI of Scotland organized the 'plantation' or colonization of Ulster, Scottish gentlemen such as Malcolm Hamilton went across to Ireland and built themselves tower houses there on the Scottish model. Hamilton built Monea Castle in County Fermanagh, and it looks remarkably like Claypotts.

The most distinctive feature of Claypotts is the way the round towers are corbelled out to bear rectangular 'cap houses' on top, looking for all the world like a pair of humble farm cottages, complete with ridge roofs and dormer windows, but hoisted up on big round pillars.

Although this is an unusual-looking building, it is a good example of a Z-plan tower house - a rectangular block with round towers at two of the diagonally opposite corners. Claypotts was not so much built as a defensive structure but a dwelling as it has only a few defensive features.

GLAMIS CASTLE

Angus

Glamis (pronounced Glahms) was built in the eleventh century as a royal hunting lodge for the Scottish kings. The name comes from the Gaelic 'glamhus', or vale. William Shakespeare famously set the murder of King Duncan I at Glamis in his Scottish play, but Shakespeare was using a great deal of dramatic licence. Duncan was not murdered there, in fact he was not murdered in his sleep at all, but died in battle. He did however meet his death in 1040, fighting against Macbeth, who was a rival claimant to the Scottish throne. Duncan's predecessor and maternal grandfather, King Malcolm II, is believed to have died there in 1034. Several later Scottish kings were to live at Glamis.

When the poet Thomas Gray stayed there in 1765 he wrote that it was 'very singular and striking in appearance, like nothing I ever saw.' The first sight to greet the visitor, framed at the end of a long and wide avenue of oak trees, is a massive and high building bristling with clusters of pointed turrets. The effect of loftiness and mass would have been enhanced before the wings lost their gabled roofs. Around the year 1800 the old gabled roofs were taken off to give them a crenellated roofline, and this was a mistake; pitched roofs with gables would harmonize better with the pointed turrets and spires.

The castle is in any case a splendid example of the 'Scottish baronial' style, an amalgam of the Scottish tower house and the French Renaissance chateau. With its seventeenth century battlements, corner turrets and conical spires it comes closer than almost any other building in Britain to a fairy-tale castle. The decorative details that give it such a distinctive skyline probably did nothing for the castle's defensive capacity, but at the core of Glamis is a stout, no-nonsense fourteenth century tower, which makes it a real castle. A fourteenth century iron yett still defends the main entrance; this device is a massive grille that replaced the portcullis.

The core of the castle dates from the fourteenth and fifteenth centuries, at which time it was surrounded by a curtain wall. In the seventeenth century it was remodelled, and the interior was decorated with fine plasterwork. It was after the Restoration that the third Earl of Strathmore and Kinghorne heightened the main block and gave it its fancy roofline.

In 1372, the castle passed to Sir John Lyon. When he married the daughter of King Robert II, his grandson became the first Lord Glamis. In the sixteenth century the castle was seized by James V, who took all its contents and ensured that Lady Glamis was burnt as a witch. There was no evidence against her, but she was a Douglas, and that was enough to make the King hate her. She was executed on Castle Hill in 1540.

It was one of the most outstandingly scandalous, cruel and unjust acts in a century that excelled in scandal, cruelty and injustice.

In the seventeenth century the Lords of Glamis acquired the Earldoms of Kinghorne and Strathmore. The fifth Earl was a close friend and follower of Montrose. The family's Stuart sympathies lingered on, and the Stuart heir to the throne of England and Scotland, who was known to the English as 'The Old Pretender', and to his followers as the Chevalier de St George or even James VIII, was entertained at Glamis Castle. Relics of the king-in-exile are still kept at the castle, including his coat, breeches, sword and watch. These eighteenth century Lords of Glamis lived in ostentatiously high style. It seems they were the very last aristocratic family in Scotland to maintain a court jester. The last jester's silken suit of motley has been preserved.

In 1767, the family made a great fortune for itself when the ninth Earl married the Durham heiress Mary Bowes; from then on the family was known as Bowes Lyon. Glamis is one of the finest private houses in Britain and it holds a special place in the affections of the British because it was where the Queen Mother spent her childhood, her honeymoon and where she gave birth to her second daughter, Princess Margaret.

Glamis is said to be the most haunted castle in the British Isles. The Grey Lady, who has been seen from time to time, is said to be the ghost of Janet Douglas who was burnt at the stake in the sixteenth century. Another ghost is that of a page-boy. He was apparently told to sit on the step and wait until the family was ready for him; he was then forgotten about and just went on sitting there. He is said to be sitting there still, tripping up passers-by for fun. Glamis has a secret chamber, but only the castle's owner knows where it is. There is even a ghost story to explain why the chamber cannot be found. One evening the Earl of Glamis and his friend were playing cards in a room in the castle. Late in the evening a page went to warn them that midnight approached and that it would be a sin to continue playing on into the sabbath. Apparently they went on playing regardless and at midnight the walls of the chamber sealed around them like a tomb. The ghosts of the Earl and his friend are said to go on and on playing cards; around midnight the sound of their game can still be heard.

Modern visitors, who naturally never visit the secret chamber, see the Dining Room first, a rare and unexpected example of untouched nineteenth century decor – in Elizabethan style. It contrasts dramatically with the barrel-vaulted crypt that lies beyond, its plain walls set with hunting trophies and weapons. Over the Crypt is the Jacobean Great Hall, which is now called the Drawing Room. The suite of Royal Apartments was arranged by the fourteenth Countess of Strathmore for her youngest daughter when she was Duchess of York; the Duchess continually returned to these apartments as Duchess, then as Queen Elizabeth, and then as Queen Elizabeth the Queen Mother.

Glamis Castle has been a royal residence since 1372. It was the childhood home of Her Majesty Queen Elizabeth The Queen Mother, birthplace of Her Royal Highness The Princess Margaret and legendary setting for Shakespeare's famous play Macbeth.

INVERARAY CASTLE

ARGYLLSHIRE

Inveraray Castle on Loch Fyne is the home of the Dukes of Argyll and its story is inextricably intertwined with theirs. As the thirteenth and present Duke, Torquhil, has said, 'Inveraray Castle is first and foremost a family home. Its very existence reflects the part my family played in the rich tapestry of Scotland's history. Many of my forebears have themselves helped to shape events of national importance.' The Campbells have been Earls of Argyll since 1457. The tenth Earl was a vigorous anti-Jacobite and the champion of William of Orange. For this he was raised to the dukedom in 1701. The Argylls' ancient stronghold was Innischonnel Castle, now a ruin, on Loch Awe. It was the third Duke, inheriting the title and the estates at the age of 60, who planned the new seat at Inveraray.

In 1743, the third Duke, Archibald, launched one of the most ambitious building projects ever seen in the Highlands of Scotland. There was a fifteenth century fortified tower house at Inveraray, and what the third Duke did was to replace it with an entirely new castle. The walls were up and the roof on within ten years. It was all completed by the time of Dr Johnson's visit in 1773. The old settlement of Inveraray, which lay across the present garden, was rebuilt further away.

Inveraray Castle is an extraordinary building. It is more like a French château than a British castle. It stands foursquare and moatless, with graceful conical spires rising from round corner towers. The facade is pure French château, but peeping over its roofline is a more rugged, battlemented superstructure that is at odds with the civilized facade. It breaks across, as if to remind us of a barbaric past. But overall Inveraray is a great house, a rich mansion. The interior reinforces this impression, though in classical style, not Gothic. There is a fine Victorian Room, which has a maplewood desk given by Queen Victoria to her daughter Princess Louise on the occasion of her marriage to the ninth Duke. The Clan Room is devoted to telling the story of the development of the Clan Campbell.

The castle was designed by the London architect Roger Morris, and the supervising architects were William and John Adam. Morris was an odd choice, as he was not a 'palace' man, though he had designed Clearwell Castle in Gloucestershire. Duke Archibald's castle was not at all Scottish; it was low, urbane, civilized and convenient. It is thought that the design may have been inspired by Sir John Vanbrugh's designs for Blenheim and Castle Howard, because like those palaces Inveraray has a large central tower lit by large high windows. The strange architecture is perfectly matched by the choice of building stone, a greenish-blue schist, which gives an exotic and otherworldly look to the building. It looks for all the world as if it were made of icing-sugar. The magnificent interiors were designed by Robert Mylne for the fifth Duke at the time of the French Revolution.

This is an early Gothic Revival castle built in the mid-eighteenth century by Roger Morris. In 1773 Dr Johnson journeyed through Scotland and visited the castle. His comment: 'What I admire here, is the total defiance of expense'.

IONA ABBEY

ARGYLLSHIRE

Iona is the site of the most important early monastery in Scotland, founded in 563 by the Irish missionary St Columba and 12 disciples. It was a day's sail away from Ireland – and a springboard for the conversion of Scotland. St Columba's biography was written by Adamnan, the ninth Abbot of Iona.

The foundation of Iona (then called 'Hy') marked the beginning of a continuous tradition of Christianity and monasticism in Scotland. The most impressive remains at this major site are of an earthwork which defines the roughly rectangular precinct. This was a dynamic and flourishing early Christian community, as is shown by the magnificent high crosses. Many early Scottish kings wanted to be buried at what came to be regarded as an exceptionally holy place.

The medieval abbey of Iona was a much later development, but it was built upon the same site as the historic monastery. Most of the original abbey church at Iona has gone, but the details of the contemporary Augustinian nunnery nearby give a guide to what it was probably like. The arcades flanking the nave were rounded Romanesque arches. The windows were round-headed and splayed, in other words the window openings were much larger on the inside than on the outside. The windows were linked by prominent string courses in the masonry. The design was essentially in a Romanesque style borrowed more from Ireland than from Scotland.

The founder of both the abbey and the nunnery was Reginald, the son of Somerled, the King of the Isles. He also founded the single Cistercian abbey in the Western Highlands of Scotland, at Saddell. Reginald founded Iona Abbey in around 1200.

The church and abbey are complete, but much of what is seen today at Iona is a result of modern restoration. Even so, the chancel and the south transept are still essentially the same as when they were remodelled in the later middle ages; the north transept has survived from the earlier building period. The remodelling involved destroying a crypt and lowering the floor level of the choir and presbytery; it also involved shortening the north aisle to make a sacristy. A new, squat tower was built over the crossing. The result is a well-proportioned, compact and serviceable building. Some of the architectural ideas were borrowed from the Scottish Lowlands, like the cylindrical columns in the south aisle, but some were taken from Ireland. An inscription on the south arcade shows that at least one Irish mason was working at Iona – a reminder that it was easier for people to reach the Western Highlands from Ireland than from the Scottish Lowlands.

The abbey of Iona was restored in recent times specifically for the Iona Community. The place has become, once again, a focus for pilgrimage, as people of all faiths, and none, come from all over the world to a place that seems to have a special sanctity.

One of Scotland's most historic and venerated sites, Iona Abbey is a celebrated Christian centre and the burial place of early Scottish kings. The Abbey and Nunnery grounds house one of the most comprehensive collections of Christian carved stones in Scotland, ranging in age from 600 AD to the 1600s.

KILCHURN CASTLE

ARGYLLSHIRE

Today, Kilchurn Castle is an imposing valley floor ruin standing on a little peninsula on the marshy banks of Loch Awe. What we see represents 250 years of thoughtful building and occupation, followed by 250 years of abandonment and neglect.

It was in about 1420 that Sir Colin Campbell of Glenorchy first built the five-storey tower house, which still stands intact at the eastern end of the site. The tower house was the standard design for a Scottish fortified home, the equivalent of the English moated manor-house. It was quite common for English castles to be entered at first-floor level, but Kilchurn was entered from the ground floor. Immediately above the vaulted entrance hall was the Great Hall, with two further storeys stacked above it to provide accommodation. At the top of the castle was an attic or garret leading out onto a parapet walk. A curtain wall, sometimes called a barmkin wall, enclosed the rest of the site; the southern stretch of this is still standing.

Early in the sixteenth century Kilchurn Castle was extended by Sir Duncan Campbell, who added a single-storey dining hall up against the inside of the south curtain wall. His descendant, another Sir Colin, the sixth Laird of Kilchurn, added some chambers to the north of the tower house and remodelled the parapet; this included adding some round corner turrets with stone corbels, which are still in position. At the end of the sixteenth century the MacGregors of Glenstrae were the occupants of the castle; they were appointed keepers of Kilchurn when the Campbells spent much of their time at Fincham. This amicable arrangement lasted until the early seventeenth century, when a violent feud between the two families brought it to an end.

In 1616 the seventh Laird of Kilchurn, Sir Duncan, added a second storey to the dining hall and extended it to join the tower house. This extension included space for a chapel. The final stage in the castle's development was the building of a range of barracks along the northern curtain wall. At the same time three round towers were added to strengthen the north, south and west corners of the curtain wall; two of these are still standing,

Kilchurn is one of those castles that by chance had a fairly trouble-free history. The only significant military incident was in 1685, when it briefly came under siege. It was garrisoned by Sir John, the first Earl of Breadalbane, while he was supporting the government against the Earl of Argyll's invasion. Kilchurn Castle was again garrisoned by government troops during later insurrections, the 1715 and 1745 Jacobite Rebellions. By that stage, the castle had been virtually abandoned by its owners, who moved to Taymouth Castle in 1740. That spelt the end for Kilchurn.

The castle quickly fell into a state of decay. First abandoned by its family, then struck by lightning in 1769 and losing its roof in 1770, the hostile elements quickly turned this carefully crafted fortress into a ruin.

ST ANDREWS CATHEDRAL & CASTLE

Fife

St Andrews was a monastery and the seat of a bishop at least as early as the eighth century, when it was known as Kinrimund. Bishop Acca was exiled from his diocese at Hexham in 732 and settled at Kinrimund, bringing with him the relics of St Andrew that gave the place its new name. The bishops of St Andrews emerged as the most important in Scotland, calling themselves Bishops of the Scots.

The cathedral that was started in 1160 is in a very ruined state, but enough fragments survive to show what at least the eastern part must have looked like. Jedburgh gives a good idea of what St Andrews looked like; the masons who built Jedburgh had earlier worked on St Andrews. An attractive feature is the intersecting arcading along the transept walls. This consists of two sets of round arches following each other like two voices singing a canon. It was at St Andrews that features such as piers made of bundles of shafts and leaf-form capitals were first used in a major Scottish church. The innovations at St Andrews were to be adopted on a large scale in both Scotland and England.

The bishops of St Andrews saw themselves as great leaders, and the addition of high vaulting over the chancel was a statement of ambition and status. The Bishop of Kirkwall copied the high vaulting in a kind of race for status.

The east gable wall stands completely intact, but with no walls attached on either side, which makes it look rather odd. There is a substantial part of the west front still standing, but nothing much in between. St Andrews Cathedral looks like a demolition site, and is far from picturesque.

As the Reformation approached, signs of decadence began to appear. In 1513, the Archbishop of St Andrews, James IV's illegitimate son, was killed at Flodden. The Pope hoped to take advantage of the crisis following Flodden by imposing his own nephew but the Scots had strong ideas of their own; there were six claimants. Eventually in 1526 it was decided that the King would nominate his candidate to the Pope, and then the Pope would tell the chapter whom to elect. Further confusion followed soon after when Henry VIII of England rejected the Pope as head of the English Church.

It was common for Scottish bishops to have their own castles. The Archbishop of St Andrews lived in a castle that was built in about 1200, destroyed, and then rebuilt by Bishop Walter Trail in the fourteenth century. Trail laid his castle out as an irregular pentagon with towers at the angles and ranges of buildings against the curtain walls. It made a handsome residence and also a formidable stronghold. But even the strongest castle could not defend a bishop against a determined siege – or against assassination. The nephew of Archbishop James Beaton, Cardinal David Beaton, was murdered in St Andrews Castle in 1546 and the castle was afterwards taken following bombardment by a French fleet.

STIRLING CASTLE

STIRLINGSHIRE

When Edward I of England invaded, Stirling Castle was reckoned to be the strongest fortress in Scotland. It was still mainly timber, yet it withstood the onslaught of the English stone-throwing engines so well that Edward was reduced to stripping the lead from cathedral roofs in order to increase the power of his catapults.

Unfortunately all trace of the castle as it was at the time of the Battle of Bannockburn in 1314 has disappeared. It was James III of Scotland (1460–88) who gave Stirling Castle its commanding dignity by giving it a central turreted gatehouse, curtain walls and flanking towers. Directly opposite the gatehouse he had a Great Hall built where parliaments and state ceremonies could be held.

Stirling Castle has an unusual layout. On the south-east side is the Counterguard, an area of outer defensive works consisting of walls, ditches and gun batteries. On the north-west side is the Nether Bailey, an enclosure with no buildings in it. Between the two is the castle proper, which consists of a palace block on the south side and three major buildings, the Great Hall, the King's Old Building and the Chapel Royal, arranged round an open space, the Upper Square.

In April 1304, after wintering at Dunfermline, Edward I began his great siege of Stirling Castle. The defenders under Sir William Oliphant held out for three months without any real hope of being relieved. The castle itself was impregnable, but the garrison had to surrender in the end because they ran out of food. In July, Oliphant and his followers marched out and were sent off to various English prisons. For the next ten years, Stirling Castle stood as a symbol of English authority, blocking communication between north and south.

In 1313, the castle came under a blockade by Edward Bruce, the brother of King Robert. Sir Philip Mowbray, the English custodian, offered to surrender if relief had not come by 24 June, 1314. Edward Bruce agreed to these terms, which alarmed his brother, who was not ready to meet the English in a pitched battle.

Edward II marched north with a huge feudal army, drawing up in sight of Stirling Castle. He sent a detachment to help the castle garrison, but this was driven back. Against all expectation, the Scots then defeated the huge English host on the nearby field of Bannockburn. The castle was surrendered to the Scots as promised, and then Robert the Bruce set about dismantling its fortifications in case the English reoccupied them, which they did shortly afterwards.

With the Stewarts on the throne, Stirling Castle once more became a royal residence. James II made the castle a dower-house for his queen, Mary, and when they were married a magnificent tournament was held below the castle walls. In 1452, James II formed the idea that William Earl of Douglas was plotting against him. He invited Douglas to Stirling, promising him safe conduct. Douglas arrived and was cordially entertained at dinner. Then the king invited Douglas to an inner chamber to confer. In this brief discussion James II asked his guest to dissolve the league of Douglas and Douglas said that he neither could nor would. In James's mind the survival of the monarchy depended on the removal of this powerful league, and he promptly stabbed the Earl. James's courtiers sprang forward to make sure the Earl was dead, and his body was flung out of the window. An enquiry into the murder acquitted the King on the grounds that the earl had been an oppressor and had refused to aid the king. These findings only fanned rebellion, and the dead Earl's brother, James, the new ninth Earl, rode up to Stirling Castle brandishing the letter of safe conduct.

James IV, who acquired the throne by rebelling against and killing his father in 1488, indulged his guilt at Stirling. He spent a lot of time in the Chapel Royal and 'was ever sad and dolorous in his mind for the death of his father.' But James IV had his lighter side. He enjoyed hunting and ensured that the royal castle garden, known as the Great Garden or the King's Knot, was well maintained. He had a new park stocked with deer, boars and wild white cattle. Cranes and peacocks stalked the castle precincts. It was the peak of Stirling Castle's medieval splendour.

One of Scotland's grandest castles due to its imposing position and impressive architecture, Stirling Castle commands the countryside for many miles around. It towers over some of the most important battlefields of Scotland's past, including Stirling Bridge, the site of William Wallace's victory over the English in 1297, and Bannockburn, where Robert the Bruce defeated the same foe in the summer of 1314.

James IV's alliance with France against England brought him into conflict with the Tudor kings of England. In April 1513 an envoy from Henry VIII arrived at Stirling Castle to try to persuade James IV to abandon his alliance with France. He refused, and five months later he spectacularly lost the Battle of Flodden – and his life.

It was at Stirling Castle that the young Mary Queen of Scots was crowned. Henry VIII's envoy acidly commented that the coronation was conducted 'with such solemnity as they do use in this country, which is not very costly.' Mary later used Stirling Castle as a stopping place on journeys north. One night when she was in bed at Stirling she set her bed curtains on fire with a candle and she was nearly overcome by the smoke. In 1566 an elaborate baptism was celebrated for her infant son, to be James VI of Scotland, costing £12,000. Expensive gifts lavished on the child included a gold font from Elizabeth I, Prince James's godmother. Torches lined the way from the nursery to the Chapel, where an archbishop and four bishops waited to perform the ceremony.

After the murder of his father and the forced abdication of his mother, the one-year-old James was crowned King James VI at Stirling, and kept under protection in Stirling Castle while the great lords struggled for power around him. In due course James VI laid on another expensive baptism, for his own son, Prince Henry. This ceremony cost the Scots £100,000 and took place in the rebuilt Chapel Royal. Prince Henry was the last Prince of Scotland to be brought up at Stirling Castle.

Once the crowns of Scotland and England were united, the glory of Stirling Castle instantly evaporated.

In the Civil War, General Monk bombarded Stirling Castle for three days in August 1651 and caused a great deal of damage. The castle was ransacked by the Parliamentarians, who took wall-hangings and 40 guns.

After the Restoration of the monarchy in 1660, the castle was returned to the Earl of Mar, though it was taken from his family by the English Crown at the time of the Jacobite rebellions when it was suspected of disloyalty. Curiously, in 1923, Stirling Castle was restored to the Earl of Mar by George V.

BORTHWICK CASTLE

MIDLOTHIAN

Of all the tower houses built in Scotland in the fifteenth century, Borthwick Castle is the one that stands out as truly exceptional. It is the largest in scale, with its 1,100m² (11,840ft²) of floor space; at a height of 36m (118ft), it is the tallest of the tower houses; it is also the most sophisticated architecturally, with high quality ashlar masonry and cleverly arranged accommodation. It represents the climax in the development of that particular type of castle.

It was in 1420 that Sir William Borthwick was granted his licence 'to construct a castle . . . and fortify the same.' Sir William must have been very proud of his castle, which was so far in advance of any other. He must also have been the envy of his peers, although he was only in the second rank of the nobility at the time when he built it; it was 20 years before he was raised to the peerage by James II, and given the title Lord Borthwick, though the grand conception of Borthwick Castle shows how ambitious he was.

Sir William's design at Borthwick seems to have been driven not just by a desire to impress but by a desire to pull all of the accommodation into a single massive tower under a single roof. The plan is a kind of E-plan with the central stem missing, or a cube with a slot cut into one side; the walls rise sheer to a level roof line on all sides, giving each floor the same outline plan. The ground and first floors consisted of store rooms, a prison and a Steward's Chamber. The second floor housed a magnificent and impressive Great Hall with a soaring 10-metre (33-foot)-high stone vault. Leading off it were kitchens on one side and a withdrawing chamber on the other. The floors above that consisted of the lord's apartments, which included a further hall and a chapel.

A curiosity of Borthwick Castle is the many masons' marks cut into the ashlar blocks. These were symbols carved into the blocks to indicate which part of the building they were intended for. There are over 60 different marks at Borthwick and, among other things, they show that the castle was built all in one go. The spiral staircases and even the kerb on the well in the basement all turn out to be part of the original design. The marks also show that several additional masons were brought in to work on the massive vaulted ceiling for the Great Hall, which was intended to be a spectacular set piece.

The masons' marks show that 20 of the masons who worked on Borthwick went on to work on the nearby Roslin Chapel, famed ever since for its highly exotic carvings. A stone's throw from this very fine castle stands St Kentigern's Church. In its south chapel there is a splendid double tomb. It is thought to be the tomb of Sir William, the first Lord Borthwick, and his wife, but by some strange oversight Sir William neglected to leave an inscription to tell us.

Borthwick Castle built in 1430, is unique and exclusive. Once the refuge of Mary Queen of Scots and the Earl of Bothwell and besieged by Oliver Cromwell in 1650, the atmosphere and grandeur of its romantic past have been lovingly cherished and maintained.

EDINBURGH CASTLE

MIDLOTHIAN

Edinburgh is dominated by its castle like few other cities. At just over 100m (328ft) high, its Castle Rock is not especially high, yet it provides the ideal location for an early medieval stronghold. From the summit there are wide views across the Lowlands of Scotland, and its near-vertical rocky crags make it the ideal defensive site. The castle was built on the highest point of a crag-and-tail, a stream-lined feature eroded by ice, and the tail gives a single gently sloping access route, Edinburgh's main street, the Royal Mile.

Edinburgh Castle was the core of the original settlement. Indeed, back in the dark ages one and a half millennia ago, the fortress on the rock was the sum total of the settlement. It was called Din Eiddyn. It seems that as early as the sixth century AD, and possibly earlier, Castle Rock was a royal stronghold. Only a few archaeological traces remain of this early phase of occupation; the original stronghold has been obliterated by later developments on the Rock. During the middle ages a town grew up outside its gates, which became the Royal Mile, the core of the old city of Edinburgh.

Within Edinburgh Castle are rooms associated with various Scottish kings and queens. The oldest of these historic chambers is the small chapel of Queen Margaret (or St Margaret) , who died in 1093 just a few weeks after her husband Malcolm III (Malcolm Canmore). The chapel's nave is 4m (13ft) long and the chancel less than 3m (10ft). There is a decorated Norman arch leading to an apse that is, unusually, semicircular inside but square outside.

Beside the chapel is the famous Mons Meg, a huge fifteenth century bombard or cannon, weighing 5 tons; it fired cannonballs 50cm (19.5in) in diameter.

Beyond the high rock where the chapel stands is the bastion of the Half-Moon Battery. This overlooks the steep slope down into Princes Street Gardens towards a distant view of the Firth of Forth. Close by is Crown Square, and on the east side of this square is the sixteenth century royal lodging containing the Crown Room where the Scottish crown jewels lie in a glass case: the crown, sceptre, sword of state and other jewels belonging to the kings and queens of Scotland – the Honours of Scotland. There are also the apartments of Mary of Guise and her daughter, Mary Queen of Scots, including a tiny bedroom lit by an oriel window; on its ceiling are many painted monograms of Mary Queen of Scots and her son, James VI, who was born there in 1566.

On the south side of the square is the fifteenth century banqueting hall, which was restored in 1888. On the west side of the square is the Naval and Military Museum, with relics of various Scots regiments. On the north side is the Scottish National Memorial, in effect a war memorial, which stands on the site of the twelfth century church of St Mary.

TANTALLON CASTLE

EAST LOTHIAN

'The Good' Sir James Douglas was a close friend of Robert the Bruce and the rise of the Douglas fortunes, including their acquisition of estates throughout Scotland, was the fruit of this friendship. When Sir James died in 1330, his heir was his nephew William, who built the powerful Tantallon Castle. He probably built the castle to mark his elevation to the peerage as the first Earl of Douglas in 1358; certainly the castle is a major statement of status.

Tantallon Castle stands impressively atop vertical cliffs, which provide natural defence on two sides. The position on a cliffed promontory gives it a magnificent view out across the North Sea. On the other two sides, to landward, are lines of ditches and walls, which define two courts or baileys. The inner court is shielded by an awesome red sandstone curtain wall, which dates from the very first building phase; it rears up behind a yawning rock-cut ditch. This impressive curtain wall was the very last to be built from new in Scotland, and it may be that William Douglas was deliberately building in an old-fashioned, retrospective style as a gesture towards the golden age of castle-building a century before.

The oddly isolated dovecote that stands forlornly in the middle of the outer ward belongs to the final phase of the castle's history as a lordly residence in the seventeenth century. In between, Tantallon Castle served as a major-fortress-residence of the Douglases for 400 years.

The massive ruined curtain wall has three ruined towers projecting from it, providing the main residential accommodation. The central tower housed the gateway down at ground level and chambers on four levels above that, where the constable lived. The north tower, the Douglas Tower, is a mighty and impressive building in its own right, rising seven storeys. This was certainly the Earl's dwelling. Immediately behind it is a two-storey block with a great hall on the upper floor, which would have been reserved for the use of the lord and his family, and a laigh or lower hall for the lower orders.

Tantallon was unusual when built and it remained unusual. In the sixteenth century, Tantallon and Craignethan were the only lordly residences in Scotland to have artillery fortifications incorporated into their structures. Tantallon was badly damaged by James V's bombardment in 1528; afterwards the structure was patched with green stone. In the Civil War of the seventeenth century an attempt was made to improve Tantallon's fortifications by adding triangular earthwork gun emplacements called ravelins; similar installations were built at Hermitage and Huntly with the intention of enabling these by now obsolete castles to withstand sieges.

Tantallon was a quite exceptional castle, a grand gesture by the newly created Earl, and building in grand retro style. His peers in the mid-fourteenth century were opting for less ambitious and less expensive residences. William himself built more modestly at another of his properties, Hermitage, which lay close to the English border; that was built in a more contemporary and fashionable way. But at Tantallon he chose to make a flamboyant gesture. It was a grandiose flaunting of a past age of chivalry.

DRYBURGH ABBEY

ROXBURGHSHIRE

Drybugh Abbey stands 6km (3.6 miles) south-east of Melrose in southern Scotland. It was founded in around 1150 by Hugo de Morville, the Constable of Scotland, who brought a community of monks from Alnwick in Northumberland. Dryburgh was the last of the Border Abbeys to be founded, and the only one to be created under the instructions of King David I. Dryburgh was built by monks of the Premonstratensian Order. The Premonstratensians, who were known as White Canons because of their white habits, focused on a contemplative, cloistered life. Dryburgh was a typical choice of location, a secluded part of the Tweed valley, a long way from busy towns. It stands in a beautiful spot, a wooded promontory with the River Tweed sweeping round it on three sides. Unfortunately, because it was in Border country, it was almost inevitable that it would become ensnared in cross-border fighting.

The layout of Dryburgh Abbey was standard – a cross-plan church with a big square tower at the crossing. The main nave was flanked by side aisles, and south of that was a large square cloister garth and a range of monastic buildings. The remains of Dryburgh are mostly Early English in style, but with some Norman work. Of the church itself, only fragments remain: the western gable, the ends of the transept, part of the choir. It does not sound much, but the remains are of wonderful architectural quality and rich in detail. The monastic buildings have survived better, including the refectory with its beautiful rose window. In the chapter house, plaster and paintwork dating from the middle ages have survived.

Various members of the Buchan family are buried in one of the chapels. Perhaps the main point of historical interest is the tomb of Sir Walter Scott in St Mary's Aisle, which is part of the north transept. Scott's mother's family, the Haliburtons, had once owned Dryburgh. Scott thought the ruins of Dryburgh were the most romantic in the world.

In spite of the large building complex, there were probably never more than about 25 canons living there.

The abbey was first attacked by the English in 1322; Edward II camped in its grounds during his retreat from Scotland and set it on fire, rendering it unusable for a time. The buildings were restored, largely with personal funding from King Robert I. There were further attacks in 1385, 1523 and 1544. Dryburgh never recovered from this last onslaught. When the Reformation came there were perhaps 12 canons left. When they died, the abbey was abandoned and passed into the ownership of the Earl of Mar.

In 1780, the Earl of Buchan bought Dryburgh and set about conserving the ruins as a landscape gardening project. Buchan was buried at Dryburgh. Rather incongruously, given the peaceful and idyllic nature of the spot, it is also the burial place of Field Marshal Earl Haig, responsible for so many deaths in the First World War. But even the incongruity of Earl Haig's grave cannot spoil the beauty of the place. It is as Scott said, the most perfect picturesque ruin imaginable.

MELROSE ABBEY

Roxburghshire

K ing David I set about reorganizing the Scottish Church with gusto. He introduced the Cistercians to Scotland at Melrose in 1136. Benefactors set up funds for treats, such as the one Robert I gave to Melrose in 1326 to allow the monks a daily helping of rice made with milk of almonds.

One of the specialities of Melrose, as at several other abbeys, was wool production. Melrose sent its wool to the Low Countries; in fact Melrose Abbey was the biggest single producer of wool in Scotland and gained special privileges from the Court of Flanders in the 1180s.

Melrose had to be rebuilt after the English attacked it in 1385, and the rebuilding was done under the authority of the English king, Richard II, who provided funding for the work. Probably he regarded southern Scotland as reconquered by this stage. The new Melrose was laid out as a larger version of the old. The quality of the new work was outstandingly high, lavishly enriched with sculpted decoration. An English mason was responsible for the window tracery, where the English Perpendicular style is visible; verticals rise through the full height of the windows and there are fairly frequent horizontal transoms. Then there is a change, and in the south transept window the verticals veer to make flowing tracery patterns; by the early years of the fifteenth century, the masons at Melrose were looking to the European mainland for inspiration, just as with the windows in the west front at St Andrews Cathedral. In fact, at Melrose a French mason helpfully included two inscriptions telling us that he was called John Morow and that he had been born in Paris. But the ambitious rebuilding launched by Richard II was never completed.

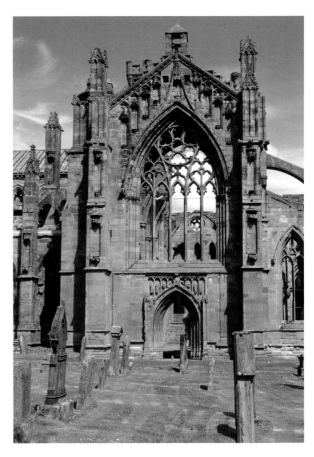

The layout of Melrose abbey was unusual, with the cloister to the north of the abbey church, as at Canterbury. Near the entrance to the refectory was the washing place, where the monks ritually washed their hands before eating. In some abbeys this was a simple trough in a wall-recess. But at Melrose there was a fountain in a special pavilion that projected into one side of the cloister.

In 1556, the abbey church was said to be becoming unusable through neglect. The Reformation was not the final blow to the abbey. There was a long period of deterioration. Fittings disappeared or were allocated to other churches. Some of these fittings were worth taking. A fifteenth century abbot was so anxious to have the very best in choir stalls that he had them imported from Bruges.

The outlines of all the main buildings at Melrose Abbey have been revealed through excavation. There are also some fine stretches of wall standing to full height to give a good impression of the building in its hey-day, like the north transept wall bearing the cloister arcading along its base. The abbey church as seen from the south-east is spectacular. Overall, Melrose is the most beautiful of all the ruins in Scotland.

JEDBURGH ABBEY

ROXBURGHSHIRE

David I of Scotland invested a huge amount of money and energy into reinvigorating the Church in Scotland. There are three churches that illustrate King David's highest architectural aspirations for the monastic Church in Scotland – Dunfermline, Kelso and Jedburgh Abbeys – built to serve three different monastic orders. Jedburgh was built for the Augustinian monks jointly by the king and his one-time tutor, Bishop John of Glasgow. At Jedburgh, David built big because this was Border country and national prestige demanded a certain amount of showing-off; he wanted to demonstrate to the English that Scottish abbeys were every bit the equal of English abbeys. The magnificent remains of Jedburgh are still overwhelmingly impressive when approached from the direction of England, just as King David intended.

Of the abbey church begun in 1138, only the western bays of the chancel and parts of the transepts survive. The original design seems to owe something to Southwell in Nottinghamshire, but Jedburgh was not a copy of any particular English abbey: it was influenced by many. The masons were even so probably brought in from southern England.

The most striking feature of the oldest part of the building is the way the two lower storeys of the chancel were embraced by giant arches carried on huge cylindrical piers. The effect is very beautiful indeed, especially given the bold and confident detailing on the arches. This was a design that originated in the choir of Tewkesbury Abbey in Gloucestershire and was later used at Romsey Abbey in Hampshire and then Glastonbury Abbey in Somerset. Some of the details imply that the masons working at Jedburgh may have travelled there directly from Tewkesbury.

The three-tiered arcaded nave at Jedburgh is magnificent. It has pillars that are clusters of eight shafts, rising to leaf-form capitals. The nave is 40 metres long and complete – except for its steeply pitched roof, and there is a clear upturned V mark on the west wall of the still-standing tower to show exactly where the absent roof should go. This building cries out to have its roof restored.

The north transept was doubled in size, and this may have been done in order to make space for extra chapels or altars at a time when there was a growing demand for prayers to be said for the dead. This transept enlargement was fairly common, and it was usually done on the side of the abbey church away from the cloister, where there were other buildings in the way, such as the chapter house or refectory.

Jedburgh was subjected to a devastating attack by the English in the 1540s, which led to a flurry of late rebuilding activity. With the benefit of hindsight, this looks like a lost cause. But interest in keeping the building alive as a piece of architecture was still there, and an awareness dawned that stripping away modern additions might allow people to appreciate the wonders of the medieval work in an abbey that was truly a masterpiece.

Jedburgh Abbey's grand design was inspired by Europe's magnificent churches, and was founded in 1138 by David I. When Anglo-Scottish relations deteriorated after 1296, Jedburgh became a frontline target for English armies. The Reformation heralded the abbey's final decline, but it was used as the local church up to 1875, after which it became disused.

CAERLAVEROCK CASTLE

DUMFRIESSHIRE

A French poem about the siege of Caerlaverock in 1300 vividly describes the castle as seen by its contemporaries; *In shape it was like a shield, for it had but three sides round it, with a tower at each corner, and strong with a drawbridge and a sufficiency of other defences. And it had good walls and good ditches filled right up to the brim with water. I think you will never see a more finely situated castle.*

Repeatedly in its history, this water-surrounded castle became entangled in the border conflict between England and Scotland. In 1300, when it was but 20 years old, it was besieged and taken by Edward I, who then held it for 12 years until the keeper of the castle switched his allegiance to Robert the Bruce. The English returned to lay siege to well-moated Caerlaverock, but this time they failed to take it. Clearly Caerlaverock was seen as an important strategic stronghold by the English, so Robert the Bruce ordered the keeper, Sir Eustace Maxwell, to dismantle it and so prevent the English from using it.

Remains of an earlier castle can be seen in the woods a few hundred metres away. The place was an important strategic point in the dark ages. Close to the head of Solway Firth, it was on the Roman road linking the two northern kingdoms of Rheged (Cumbria) and Clyde (South-west Scotland). In 573 the great Battle of Arderydd (Arthuret) was fought at Longtown. The battle was remembered in the Welsh Triads as one of the Three Futile Battles: 'the action of Arderydd, which was brought about by the cause of the lark's nest.' This cryptic comment can be explained. Caerlaverock means 'the fortress of the lark', or more poetically, 'the lark's nest'. The battle was therefore remembered as being fought for possession of the Scottish shore of the Solway Firth.

King Gwenddolau was master of Caerlaverock then, and he was one of the leading combatants who died in the battle in and round his own fortress. Gwenddolau had a bard like other kings, but his bard was called Myrddin, which makes us look more closely at him. Myrddin fought in the battle alongside his master. When he saw his lord killed, he went mad and became a hermit in the Wood of Celidon. Myrddin was undoubtedly the prototype for the 'Merlin' who was later alleged to have been Arthur's bard. Castles and especially ruined castles seem to attract swirling histories and legends round their weathered stones. Warriors and wraiths are equally part of their story. Caerlaverock is especially rich in this layering of past and possibility. It is hauntingly strange to think of Merlin's historical predecessor, Myrddin, fighting in a pitched battle under the walls of Caerlaverock Castle's predecessor. And how much stranger still to think of him running off into the woods grief-stricken and distraught, suffering from a dark age version of shell-shock.

Surrounded by a double moat and hundreds of acres of flat marshy willow woods Caerlaverock Castle was built to control the South-West entrance to Scotland which in early times was the waterway across the Solway Firth.

SWEETHEART ABBEY

DUMFRIESSHIRE

Sweetheart Abbey was named by the abbey's monks in honour of the founder, Lady Devorgilla. She had the monastery built in 1275 in memory of her husband King John de Balliol, and had his embalmed heart kept there in a casket of silver and ivory. When she too died, in 1289, she was buried in front of the high altar, with her husband's heart.

It was a very fine Early English church 60m (200ft) long with a central tower 28m (92ft) high. The monastic buildings were on the same large scale and surrounded by an enclosure wall of granite 3m (1ft) high.

Sweetheart Abbey stands in tranquil rural scenery, but it is also in Border country, which put it in the path of invading English armies. In 1300, Edward I of England, the Hammer of the Scots, stayed at Sweetheart after sacking Caerlaverock Castle, which belonged to the Maxwells, Sweetheart Abbey's great benefactors. It was while staying at Sweetheart Abbey that Edward I heard that there was a demand from the Pope to stop his oppression of the Scots. This led to a truce and Edward's return to England late in 1300. Later, Lady Devorgilla's son John Balliol would be Edward I's nominee for the Scottish throne.

Unlike other Border abbeys, Sweetheart Abbey did not suffer from the English invasions, and it continued as a place of worship – even through the Reformation. When the Lords of the Congregation ordered that the abbey must be destroyed in 1560, the sixth Lord Maxwell refused, saying that he was attached to the place where he was brought up.

Sweetheart Abbey's final years were spent under its best-known superior, Abbot Gilbert Broun, who went on upholding the Catholic faith long after the Reformation. He lived at the Maxwells' Kirkconnell House until 1605, in a building known as the Abbot's Tower. He was repeatedly denounced for being a papist, and was seized by his enemies and banished in 1605. The last monks were forced to leave Sweetheart in 1608.

Then the great abbey became a quarry for those who wanted ready-shaped stone for building. The piecemeal destruction continued for 200 years, and only stopped in the nineteenth century when some local people acquired the property and stopped its deterioration. Thanks to this intervention, the ruins are substantial. The nave, the bell tower, the masonry of the great east window are all intact. There are also the most complete precinct walls to be found at any Scottish monastery.

At the red broken heart of the abbey ruins is a reminder of the love story that led to the building of the abbey over 700 years ago, an effigy of Lady Devorgilla, holding the casket containing her husband's heart. It is a touching image of the same kind as the famous Arundel tomb in Chichester Cathedral, where the effigies of a medieval knight and his wife lie side by side, forever holding each other's stone hands.

KIRKWALL CATHEDRAL

ORKNEY

'. . . build a stone minster at Kirkwall more magnificent than any in Orkney, that you'll have (it) dedicated to your uncle the holy Earl Magnus and provide it with all the funds it will need to flourish. In addition, his holy relics and the episcopal seat must be moved there.'
The Orkneyinga Saga
Chapter 68

There were bishops in Orkney before 1035, overseeing a Norse-controlled diocese, and it is thought by some that they had their cathedral at Birsay, at the north-western tip of Mainland Orkney. The site of the secular power base on the island, the Brough of Birsay, has been explored by archaeologists, and it has yielded a great deal about the home of the Norse chieftains of Orkney, though nothing that could credibly be identified as an early cathedral. Kirkwall, nearer the centre of Mainland Orkney, may well not have been the obvious choice for a Norse cathedral, and the site of a cathedral at Birsay may yet be discovered.

Most Scottish cathedrals were built on a fairly modest scale. This is surprising, in that by the mid-twelfth century abbeys were being built on a large scale, which proved that large buildings were feasible. In terms of size, Kirkwall Cathedral was an exception, and this may be because when most of the building was done Orkney was not actually in Scotland; along with the rest of the Northern Isles, Orkney was part of Norway and did not become part of Scotland until the fifteenth century.

Kirkwall Cathedral was built in the eleventh century and then rebuilt in 1137, and it was the first cathedral in what is now Scotland to be built on a grand scale. The decision to build big was made by Earl Rognvald of Orkney, the nephew of the martyred St Magnus, who had been treacherously murdered on Egilsay, one of the smaller islands to the north of Mainland Orkney. The Norse earldom of Orkney was shared between Magnus Erlendsson and his cousin Hakon. After years of feuding they agreed to hold a peace meeting on Egilsay in 1117. Hakon treacherously seized Magnus and had him executed. Magnus's composure during this ordeal earned him his canonization. A cult developed, and his kinsman Rognvald had the new cathedral built in his honour.

Building Kirkwall Cathedral was a massive project, almost beyond the grasp of a relatively small community, and it was not completed by the Reformation. Work began at the east end, so that services could be held as soon as possible in the unfinished building. The chancel was to be of two aisled bays terminating in a semi-circular apse for the high altar and the shrine of St Magnus. The short transepts had no aisles but probably had chapel-apses on their east walls. The aisled nave was eventually to be eight bays long, though probably initially it was not intended to be so long. A tower was raised over the crossing.

Internally, Kirkwall Cathedral was built in three storeys. Below there were tall round-arched arcades on plain drum-shaped pillars. These carried a middle tier of round-arched arcades opening into galleries between the stone vaults and the roofs over the side aisles. At the top level was the clerestorey, with windows letting light into the central space and

Internally, Kirkwall Cathedral was built in three storeys. Below there were tall round-arched arcades on plain drum-shaped pillars. These carried a middle tier of round-arched arcades opening into galleries between the stone vaults and the roofs over the side aisles.

a passage let into the thickness of the walls. To begin with there was a wooden roof, but this was later replaced with a stone vault.

The plan and many of the details seem to copy Dunfermline Abbey and probably both churches employed masons who had worked on Durham Cathedral. Even though Kirkwall was still a part of the Norwegian Church, what happened there was strongly influenced by what was happening not just in Norway and Scotland but in England too.

The massive work of the first phase at Kirkwall is entirely Romanesque in style and spirit. When the transepts were modified later, the mouldings used were thinner, pointed and distinctly Early English in style. The visually heavy cushion capitals and scalloped capitals of the Romanesque phase were replaced by capitals covered in foliage. These forward-looking developments were brought in by a new bishop, Biarne Kolbeinsson, elected in 1188.

The status of Kirkwall as the cathedral of the Northern Isles was marked by the installation of high stone vaulting over the choir. The only other Scottish cathedral to have high vaulting over its eastern limb was St Andrews, and there it was part of a bid by its bishops to assert their leadership of the Scottish Church. The design details of

Kirkwall and other cathedrals can therefore tell us much, if in code, about the church politics of the time.

Once the decision had been taken to give the chancel a high vault, vaulting had to be carried on down the nave, and this may be why the cathedral took so long to finish. In the thirteenth century, Kirkwall's ambitious bishops made another eloquent statement in the design of their west front. There were three doorways, two smaller flanking doorways for the side aisles, and a larger central one for the nave. The side doorways were given elaborately moulded arches carried on three free-standing shafts on each side. The central doorway was given more opulent treatment, with seven free-standing columns on each side. Probably there was going to be an elaborate carved superstructure over the doorway – a large triangular space is waiting for it – but it was unfortunately never completed. Even so, the west doors are imposing.

When the Northern Isles were pledged to Scotland by Norway in 1472, the diocese came under the new archdiocese of St Andrews, which brought to an end the ambitions of the bishops of Kirkwall; they had been demoted.

The great watershed for the Scottish Reformation was the Parliament of 1560, which rejected the Pope as head of the Church in Scotland. The Bishop of Kirkwall went along with the new arrangement. The post-Reformation histories of the cathedrals varied a great deal, but all were 'cleansed' of the trappings of medieval Catholic worship.

Of the 13 medieval cathedrals in Scotland, only five are now intact and complete, and of those, three are only complete because of substantial rebuilding in the nineteenth and twentieth centuries. That leaves only Glasgow and Kirkwall. The medieval design of Kirkwall was still unfinished by the twentieth century, and the vaulting over the west bays of the nave was only completed in the 1970s – in fibreglass.

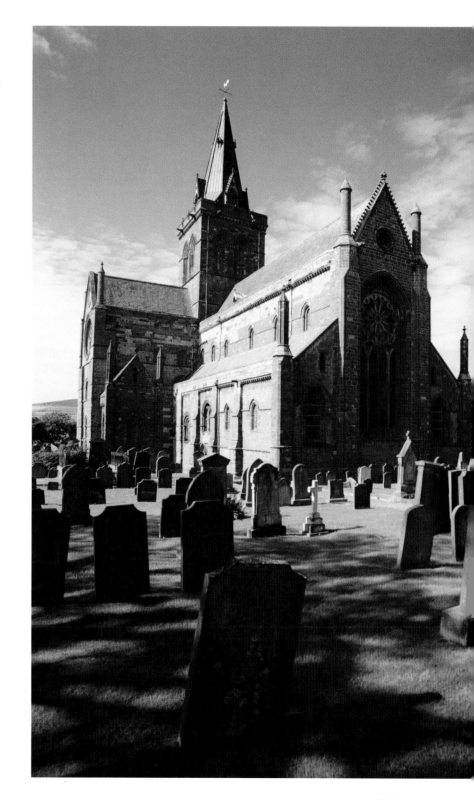

BEAUMARIS CASTLE

ANGLESEY

It was in 1295 that building work started on this castle. 'Beau Mareys' is a Norman French phrase meaning 'fair marsh'. Marshes were understandably often shunned for settlement because they were damp and seen as a source of ague (malaria), but they were certainly ideal for defence. Attackers could march or ride across dry land, or use boats across water, but there was no quick or efficient way of getting heavily armed men across a marsh. Northampton Castle similarly had the benefit of having a marshy floodplain on two sides. This is often overlooked as most of the marshes have been drained and we forget that the marshes were ever there.

Beaumaris Castle came late in the sequence of great castles of oppression built on the orders of Edward I, at a time when money was short. Beaumaris Castle was the last in the sequence, yet still designed by King Edward's chief military architect, Master James of St George. Master James had learned a great deal from designing the earlier castles, and Beaumaris was set to be his masterpiece.

The building of Beaumaris Castle began immediately after the Welsh rising under Madog ap Llewellyn had been suppressed. The new castle was to be added to the Ring of Stone the English king already had in place to throttle Welsh resistance. At the peak of the building project, Beaumaris employed 2,600 men. Building a castle was an expensive undertaking and by 1298 the funds required for completion had run out, and the work had to stop. Building began again between 1306 and 1330, but with both the work force and the design at a reduced scale. Edward I was dead and his lavish scheme was never to be completed.

The luxurious accommodation planned for the gatehouse on the north side was never finished, and it remained single-storey. The block that had been planned for the south gatehouse never got beyond its footings. Turrets had been planned for the big round corner towers. It seems that the domestic range, with the hall, kitchens and stables, was never built.

Beaumaris Castle has a symmetrical and concentric layout. A very wide moat surrounds the large square curtain wall which rises straight out of the water, as at Bodiam. Walls rising straight from the moat were harder for attackers to climb; they also looked taller and more imposing because of the reflection. The outer curtain wall was relatively low-slung. The inner defences were built higher and more massive, so that defenders could fire out over the heads of those manning the outer walls. At the southern end of the moat there was a tidal dock to deal with shipping, and this was protected by the shooting deck on Gunners' Walk.

Beaumaris Castle is a strange and beautiful building, frozen at the time of its non-completion. It was never finished and never really used. Beaumaris Castle was wonderfully designed and it would have been virtually impregnable, but it was never put to the test.

CAERNARVON CASTLE

Caernarvon is Wales's Windsor, standing as a mighty symbol of the greatness of the English monarchs. As such, this castle holds the history of Wales in a steely grip. It was begun in 1283 at the orders of Edward I, to be one of a chain of castles to subdue and control the Welsh.

Caernarvon stands at the south-western end of the Menai Strait, the sleeve of water separating Anglesey from the mainland of North Wales. It was an excellent choice of location. Anglesey was the garden of Wales, providing agriculturally rich land and therefore a reliable food supply, close to the otherwise poor land of North Wales. The Menai Strait also allowed swift access by sea to the coasts of North Wales and West Wales; from there it was possible for Edward I's forces to move quickly to Conwy or Harlech. Like all the other castles in Edward's Iron Ring, Caernarvon was built on the shoreline, to ensure the safe delivery of supplies. Although there were roads across Wales, the Welsh were good at ambush and other guerrilla warfare. Locating castles by the sea, the English could be fairly sure they would not be cut off.

Caernarvon had its origins in a Roman fort, Segontium, which was set up on a low hill to the south-east of the present town. After the Romans withdrew from Britain, in 380–90, the fort was occupied by local chieftains. Later the district round it became one of the 'manors' of the princes of Gwynedd. In the dark ages it was Conwy that emerged as the seat of the kings of Gwynedd, but Edward I selected Caernarvon as the capital of the principality of North Wales. This marked it out as a key political and military centre, and it explains why Edward wanted Caernarvon Castle to be special.

Before Edward I's masterpiece was built, a Norman motte and bailey castle had stood on the site. It was raised around the year 1090. This motte was incorporated into the later medieval fortress, but was unfortunately destroyed in 1870. The Welsh recaptured the original motte in 1115 and kept it until Edward I's invasion and colonization of 1283. The work at Caernarvon began in May 1283, after Edward's march into North Wales from Chester. Edward's intention was to create a nucleus of English influence in this area, which was one rich in Welsh tradition and anti-English feeling. Caernarvon was to be a colony settlement.

Edward I is known for the building of Caernarvon Castle. What is less often remembered is that he destroyed the Welsh town that stood beside it and replaced it with an English town. This was ruthless conquest with a vengeance.

Materials for building the castle and town were brought in by sea. The first recorded entry of the project, on 24 June, 1283, was the digging of the castle's new ditch. The next step was to raise a wooden palisade to protect the building work from attack.

The main priority in the first building phase was to make the site defensible. The walls of the castle and the town were more or less completed by the end of 1285. The remarkably gifted architect of this first phase was Edward I's chief castle builder, Master James of St George.

By the end of the first building phase, the north side of the castle still had no wall; it was instead defended by the town wall and a rock-cut ditch. Madog ap Llewellyn used this weak point to attack the castle in his rebellion of 1294. The English had little difficulty in retaking Caernarvon Castle the following summer and it was made defensible again; repairs were made and the north curtain wall of the castle was finally built, including the King's Gate.

The great castle was not completed until the reign of Edward II, in 1322, by which time it looked much as it does today, the conception of a single military mind – Master James of St George. It had cost £25,000 to build, and was easily the grandest, noblest castle Edward I had built. The Welsh hated Caernarvon Castle and the English oppression that it symbolized.

Other great castles of the Iron Ring, Harlech and Beaumaris, were concentric, consisting of two rings of defensive walls, one within the other. Caernarvon consisted of but one curtain wall, but in a sense it was concentric – the outer wall was the town wall. Caernarvon was not just for show; Master James ensured that it was as impregnable as his other castles.

The castle had two gateways. It also had seven towers punctuating its curtain wall. The King's Gate in the north wall was never completely finished, but it was still immensely strong. It was twin-towered, and was originally intended to have a drawbridge, five doors, an incredible six portcullises, to say nothing of murder holes, spy holes and arrow loops. The Queen's Gate was only slightly less formidably defended. The final, and major, segment of Caernarvon's defences was the wall of the town itself. This was a circuit 800m (875yds) long with eight towers and just two twin-towered gateways. The town walls were entirely surrounded by water-filled moats, rivers and the Menai Strait.

Originally a wall across the centre of the enclosed area divided it into two wards. Originally there were interior residential buildings, arranged round the curtain wall, but these were later destroyed. In spite of these losses, Caernarvon Castle is still among the best preserved castles in the British Isles.

The towers provided accommodation on several storeys. Two halls were built, the Great Hall and a further hall in the King's Tower. The castle was designed to be able to accommodate the king's eldest son and all his household. It was Edward I's brilliant idea to create his own son 'Prince of Wales', as if conferring a great favour on the Welsh, while in fact pulling the rug from under the feet of the native princes.

All of this was designed to turn Caernarvon into the capital of a new dominion. I compared Caernarvon with Windsor, and Caernarvon was planned as the seat of a great dynasty, the line of the new Prince of Wales. It was to be a stronghold, a royal palace, and a symbol of English dominion over Wales. Edward I was conscious of what this most spectacular of all castles would look like. The walls were given a prominent patterning with bands of different coloured stone. The towers were given angular rather than circular ground plans. Edward I was making yet another powerful symbolic statement. The thirteenth century walls of Caernarvon Castle bear a striking resemblance to the fifth century walls of Constantinople. Those who had seen Constantinople would have known that Edward I was making a bold statement at Caernarvon; this castle and this city were the heart of a powerful empire.

Material for the building of the castle, town, walls, gates and important quay were ferried in by sea. All of the initial building took place as a single operation, started in the summer of 1283. The first recorded entry (June 24th) of work was on the new castle's ditch, separating the castle from the fortified town.

CONWY CASTLE

CAERNARFONSHIRE

Conwy Castle is by any standards one of the great fortresses of medieval Europe. Along with Harlech and Caernarvon, Conwy ranks among the most impressive of all the castles in Wales. All three were designed by Master James of St George. Conwy differs from Harlech in having a well-preserved town wall. A similar town wall was built at Caernarvon but it is far less complete and is rather lost amid the later developments of the modern town. Conwy's town wall gives its town a very distinctive, indeed unique, medieval flavour that other Welsh castle towns have lost.

Work began on the construction of Conwy Castle in 1283, when it was conceived as an important link in Edward I's strategy to surround Wales with an Iron Ring of castles. As at Caernarvon, Edward I set up a colony settlement at Conwy, and the town wall was necessary to defend the incoming English settlers from the native Welsh population, who naturally opposed the colonization violently. In the town square at Conwy stands a poignant statue of Llewellyn the Great, the heroic Welsh leader and founder of Welsh Conwy who died in 1240, 40 years before the English king arrived to take it over.

It was during Edward I's second campaign in Wales that he gained control of the Conwy valley, in March 1283. Work began on the new fortress immediately, and Master James, who was Master of the King's Works in Wales, must have worked very fast indeed to produce the design for the building work to have started so quickly. A much older fortress stood on the hill on the opposite side of the Conwy estuary, Castell Degannwy. This was a fortress in the iron age and was later reoccupied and refortified as the stronghold of King Maelgwn in the middle of the sixth century; it continued to be used through the middle ages until the castle was built at Conwy. The site chosen by Edward I in discussion with Master James was a better defensive site, and the low-altitude location was more suitable for the garrison-town that was to stand beside the new castle, all to be surrounded by a town wall.

Conwy Castle and the town wall were built in a frenzy of activity in just four years, between 1283 and 1287, involving 1,500 craftsmen and labourers. Master James may have abandoned the very successful concentric design because of the restricted nature of the site, as at Caernarvon. The texture of the rock outcrop chosen for the site dictated a linear shape, with a barbican at each end. Again as at Caernarvon, the enclosure was divided in two by a cross-wall to create two separate wards. This was a precaution against the breaching of the curtain wall; if either ward should be penetrated by attackers, the other could be held as an independent stronghold.

When they were finished, the masonry walls were covered with a plastered and whitewashed rendering. This would have made the castle dazzlingly conspicuous in the

landscape, adding a further layer of intimidation to the rebellious Welsh. It would also have had the practical value of concealing the joints and courses in the masonry, along with any other weak points that the attackers might exploit. Some fragments of this medieval rendering can still be seen on the walls.

Most visitors approach Conwy from the east, from the direction of England, and the castle seems to jump up suddenly out of the hills. The much later, but still majestic, suspension bridge that connects the castle with the main peninsula guards the main entrance to the castle. The castle dominates the approach to Conwy, conveying an impression of great strength and compactness. Like Caernarvon, Conwy consists of a single large walled enclosure, by contrast to the concentric design seen at Beaumaris. The huge curtain wall surrounding the castle connects eight huge towers, all still intact. The design forms a rectangle, which is an unusually regular plan for an Edwardian castle.

Conwy Castle has a very unified and strong design. Its towers are almost identical, four on the north, four on the south, nailing the castle to the living rock. The north front is particularly striking. The towers are evenly spaced, dividing the curtain wall into three exactly similar segments, each pierced with a pair of arrow loops and all rising to the same battlement line. It is still possible to tour the wall-walks and climb from them to the tops of the towers; from these vantage points it is possible to appreciate the castle's layout.

The Inner Ward contains the suite Master James built for King Edward and Queen Eleanor in 1283. In each range the main rooms were on the first floor above dark basements. Unfortunately all the floors have now gone.

The town wall is remarkably well preserved, surviving round almost the entire circuit of the town. Only one short section is inaccessible, near the quay, and even there it still exists, incorporated into later buildings. A spur wall sticking out 60m (200ft) from the end of the quay gives some excellent views of the castle. It is 1.4km (0.8 miles) long and links together 21 towers and three twin-towered gateways. As at Caernarvon, the town wall should be regarded as part of Master James's integral design; in spite of appearances, Conwy is functionally concentric.

Edward I was besieged at Conwy during Madog ap Llewellyn's rebellion in 1295. The walls stood firm, proving the high quality of Master James's design and workmanship, though food supplies ran low. Eventually, in 1403, Conwy Castle was taken, though by trickery rather than any weakness in the castle's architecture, and it fell to the army of the Welsh leader Owain Glendower. He later sold the castle back to the English because he was running low on funds; it would have been better if he had held onto it. After the Civil War, like many other castles, Conwy was left to the elements.

PENRHYN CASTLE

CAERNARFONSHIRE

Penrhyn Castle, not far from Bangor, was built in the nineteenth century for George Hay Dawkins-Pennant, the Welsh quarry owner who had made millions out of slate. It was an age when new men became fantastically rich on the back of the Industrial Revolution, and these new men wanted new houses with which to make their mark. Yet Penrhyn Castle as ordered by Mr Dawkins-Pennant was not the first great house to stand on the site. Long before the nineteenth century re-build, in the fourteenth century, Penrhyn had been the original home of the Tudor dynasty. The genuinely medieval mansion owned by the Tudors was reconstructed as a fake-medieval house in 1782 by Samuel Wyatt.

Sir Walter Scott's romantic medieval novel *Ivanhoe* was published in 1820, and in its wake came a revolution in taste; there was a Norman Revival. Thomas Hopper was commissioned by George Hay Dawkins-Pennant to do a Norman make-over of Penrhyn Castle. Hopper was a very versatile architect, working on the principle that 'it is an architect's business to understand all styles and be prejudiced in favour of none.' It was a principle he lived by, too. At Kentwell Hall in Suffolk, and at about the same time, Hopper produced a convincing Elizabethan pastiche for another of his clients, Robert Hart Logan.

For his Normanized Penrhyn Castle, Hopper imported quantities of hard grey Mona Marble from Anglesey, and he conscientiously kept to a Norman decorative scheme throughout. The keep is colossal, 35m (115ft) high and 19m (62ft) wide, a big sombre building that Hopper modelled on the keep at Rochester Castle in Kent. Rather oddly, the monumental keep does not stand in the middle of the complex, surrounded by baileys and curtain walls, but on its own at one end of the range of buildings, stranded a little like the Great Tower at Balmoral. There is a round Ice Tower, a barbican and walls that might if necessary be defended. Hopper took his brief very seriously, even designing the library and drawing room in Norman style.

He made use of the material on which the family fortune was founded, slate, in a very unusual way. He had a mock Jacobean four-poster bed carved out of a 4-ton block of slate, as a tribute to the source of Mr Dawkins-Pennant's wealth, but even that caprice had to have Norman mouldings. Thomas Hopper was nothing if not thorough, and in a characteristically Victorian way. Did the Normans sleep on slate beds? Even if not, the decorative scheme had to be relentlessly pursued. This unusual bed was offered to Queen Victoria when she stayed at Penrhyn in 1851. Somewhat daunted, she politely turned down the offer of the slate bed; 'It is interesting but uninviting.'

The end result of Thomas Hopper's endeavour was a great showpiece, an extravaganza, and a stunning tribute to the power of Scott's novel.

HARLECH CASTLE

MERIONETH

In Welsh mythology, Harlech is linked with the tragic heroine Branwen, daughter of Lyr. The real Harlech, the Harlech of solid grey stone, is the epitome of the medieval fortress, foursquare, with a massive round tower at each corner, and steep craggy slopes falling away on three sides. Originally, the steep slope to the west dropped straight down to the sea, though now the accumulating sands of Morfa Harlech have left both castle and crag far from the sea, stranded and land-locked. Yet Harlech is still commanding; no castle in Britain has a finer site.

Harlech has clean and simple lines that are at the same time majestic and impregnable. It must have been even more striking when newly built in the reign of Edward I, with two high curtain walls, dazzlingly whitewashed. The castle was designed and created by Master James of St George, a military architect of pure genius. It was Master James who designed Beaumaris too. He adapted the Harlech site to make it into a perfect fortress, as part of King Edward's campaign to gain control over Snowdonia by throwing round it an Iron Ring of castles. These castles eventually stretched from Flint in the north-east, right round the coast to Aberystwyth in the south-west. This ambitious castle-building project was intended to prevent the region from ever becoming a focus for rebellion again.

After the Welsh stronghold of Castell y Bere fell, King Edward's army arrived at Harlech in April 1283, and Master James started building almost immediately, with a pioneer troupe of 20 quarrymen and masons. Over a six year period, Master James organized an ever-larger team of workers until there was an army of 950 quarrymen, labourers, masons and carpenters working on the site, building Harlech Castle at high speed. Unusually, this castle was built all in one go, to a single

unified design. The design was concentric, with one curtain wall set within the other. Unfortunately the outer wall is badly ruined and so no longer conveys the full effect of Master James's thirteenth century plan.

The site chosen for the castle was perfectly defended by natural cliffs on three sides, with a rocky precipice falling to the sea on the west side. It was only the east face that was open to any possible attack from the Welsh. On this side, the gatehouse juts forbiddingly forward, defying attack from the town. The townspeople must have wondered what was happening to them as this monster was born on their doorstep.

Inside the gatehouse, the gate-passage was defended by a succession of seven obstacles, including no fewer than three portcullises. Guardrooms flanked the

Even after seven centuries, Harlech Castle remains a testament to the architect, Master James of St. George. He adapted the natural strength of the site to the defensive requirements of the age, and created a building which combines a marvellous sense of majesty with great beauty in its structure and form.

passage. On the upper floors there was accommodation for the constable or governor. From 1290 to 1293 that constable was none other than Master James. Probably the rooms on the top floor of the gatehouse were for distinguished visitors, including the king himself.

Inside the castle's inner curtain wall, there is a surprisingly small and cramped inner ward. A lot of this space would have been taken up with domestic buildings – a chapel and bakehouse against the north wall, a granary against the south wall. There were also a great hall and kitchens; all of these domestic buildings have crumbled away through long neglect. The overall effect when all these buildings were standing must have been very cramped and claustrophobic, with the curtain wall and its towers rising 20 or more metres above them on all sides. The four corner towers provided more accommodation.

There is a very fine wall-walk round the battlements of the castle, giving marvellous views in all directions. An unusual feature of Harlech Castle is the 'Way from the Sea'. This is a gated and fortified staircase that plunges from the castle 60m (200ft) down to the foot of the crag. Originally, this led to the sea, which washed the foot of the rock, and enabled stores to be carried safely up to the castle from ships, but the build-up of sand has left both stairway and castle stranded.

During the rising of Madog ap Lewellyn in 1294-5, this fortified stairway saved the garrison, which was victualled by ships from Ireland. The castle was so well designed that it was possible for only 37 men to defend it.

Harlech played a major role in the Welsh rising led by Owain Glendower. Glendower laid siege to Harlech, which finally fell to him in 1404, though only through treachery, when the French fleet cut off the supply route by sea. After that, Glendower decided to make Harlech his own residence and headquarters. It is one of the places to which he summoned parliaments of his supporters. After a further siege, a reverse siege of the Welsh by the English this time, Harlech Castle was retaken by the English army in 1408. The English army was led by John Talbot, Earl of Shrewsbury. It is said that Owain Glendower had himself crowned Prince of Wales in Harlech Castle.

Later in the fifteenth century, during the Wars of the Roses, Harlech Castle was held by a Welsh chieftain called Dafydd ap Jevon ap Einion for the Lancastrians for a time, then taken by Sir Richard Herbert of Raglan for the Yorkists after a long siege. It was the endurance of this long siege that was the inspiration for the song, Men of Harlech. Dafydd held out for seven years until famine forced him to give in. A chronicler wrote, 'Kyng Edward was possessed of alle Englonde, excepte a castelle in Northe Wales called Harleke.'

In the Civil War, even though the castle had fallen into 'great decaye', it held out once again in a long siege in support of Charles I, before submitting to the Parliamentarian army of General Mytton. It was the last castle to fall, which bears remarkable testimony to the wonderful engineering of Master James, the great French 'ingeniator'. It is incredible that a thirteenth century castle could withstand the weaponry of the seventeenth century, after over 300 years of development in military technology.

The Castle wall-walks offer superb views in all directions.

CHIRK CASTLE

DENBIGHSHIRE

hirk Castle is a 700 year old marcher fortress, commanding fine views across the surrounding countryside. It was built in the thirteenth century and granted to Roger Mortimer, who was Edward I's Justice of North Wales. The great campaign by Edward I to subdue Wales hinged on local control from castles. In Edward's ambitious and ultimately highly successful scheme there were four groups of castles. There were the existing royal border castles, like Chester; there were captured native Welsh castles, like Criccieth; and there were the ten spectacular and very expensive new royal castles, such as Caernarvon. The fourth group was the new 'Lordship' castles, and there were just four of these: Denbigh, Hawarden, Holt and Chirk. These were in law to be held in private hands, but they were built to royal architectural specifications, and the building work was both supervised and subsidized by the Crown. So Chirk Castle belongs to this rather unusual category of Lordship castles, which were marcher lordships to hold the Welsh border country.

The castle has an unusual profile, a relatively low, two-storey building with smooth battlements. The round towers and bastions are broad and squat and do not rise above the general roofline. The overall look of the castle is not unlike the baldly functional Henrician forts that were built along the English Channel coast in the early sixteenth century. Chirk was held for Charles I by the former Parliamentary commander Sir Thomas Myddelton in the Civil War. Once taken it proved exceptionally difficult for the Parliamentarians to slight it; General Lambert had to use enormous amounts of gunpowder to bring down one curtain wall complete with towers.

Chirk Castle was afterwards restored and is once again intact, though as a mansion with a rectangular plan including four impressive drum-shaped towers. The magnificent iron gates at the castle entrance were made in 1718. The gates are overwhelming in their size, baroque detail and barbaric splendour, and frankly inappropriate for the rather modest and understated building that Chirk Castle is. The coat-of-arms of the Myddelton family is the focal feature of the overthrow of the gates. This coat-of-arms features the red bloody hand of the Myddeltons, three wolves' heads and an eagle's head. There are various legends to explain the red hand. One story tells of one of the early Myddeltons who was dressed in a white tunic or surcoat; he badly injured his hand during a battle and clasped it to his surcoat to staunch the bleeding. Later, he found he had left the imprint of the bloody hand on his surcoat. It was like a heraldic device, so he adopted it as one.

The design for the surrounding parkland was produced by William Emes, the landscape architect who designed the gardens at the Old Rectory, Hawarden.

Chirk was sold for £5,000 to Sir Thomas Myddelton in 1595; his descendants still live in part of the castle today.

The spirit of the fourteenth century structure is preserved in the Adam's Tower, which has a magnificent dungeon on two levels and a number of upper rooms clearly showing the 5m- (16ft-) thick walls. Two of them contain 'murder holes', through which material could be poured on to anyone trying to batter or burn down the doors below.

VALLE CRUCIS ABBEY

An isolated column known as Eliseg's Pillar stands beside the road to Ruthin above Llangollen. It was a monument to a dark age prince of Powys, and gave its name to the valley – and to the abbey built in it – Valle Crucis, the Valley of the Cross.

The abbey was founded by Madoc ap Gruffydd Maelor, who was the Lord of Castell Dinas Bran, which stands on the heights overlooking Llangollen. Madoc ap Gruffydd Maelor had spent his life fighting and plundering. By 1201, he had decided to spend some of his wealth founding an abbey, where he himself would eventually be buried. He traced his descent from the prince of Powys commemorated by Eliseg's Pillar.

The abbey was to be built down in the bottom of a deep and steep-sided valley, like Tintern, beside a tributary of the River Dee. The building was very plain and austere, with no ornaments other than carved capitals. It was also built on a smaller scale than the great Cistercian abbeys in England.

The founder's son, Gryffydd ap Madoc Maelor, married an English woman, Emma, the daughter of Lord Audley. Gryffydd sided with Henry III in his campaign to subjugate the Welsh. As a result of this extraordinary piece of treachery, Gryffydd had to steer clear of his countrymen, and retreated to his hill-top fortress; when he died, he too was buried in the abbey, which by that time had been damaged in a disastrous fire.

The rebuilding was done to a higher standard in ashlar instead of rubble. The west wall of the nave is complete, with a fine door and great triple window over it and a pretty rose window like a cartwheel above that; it is a beautiful ruin in itself. The chapter house was rebuilt, with vaulted aisles and decorated windows, and this has remained more or less intact. The chapter house at Valle Crucis is in fact one of the best and certainly one of the

best preserved Cistercian chapter houses in Britain. A hundred years ago there was still glass in its windows. There were also ash trees growing amongst the foundations and ivy growing over the fabric of the building; these were unfortunately damaging the structure of the building, but they greatly enhanced its character. Now the ruin looks bleak, bare, bald.

After the Dissolution Valle Crucis Abbey was granted to Sir William Pickering. He made a house out of the east range, insensitively facing the chimney breast with a grave slab. When George Borrow visited Valle Crucis he was unimpressed with a church that was 'roofless and had nothing remarkable about it, save the western window, which we had seen from without.'

In its hey-day, Valle Crucis had much more to offer. The fifteenth century bard Guttyn Owain praised the abbey's hospitality. He dined on four meat courses from silver dishes and served with claret, at a table with an abbot who wore rings on his fingers. It was a life style that was a long way from the ascetic rule of the early Cistercians – and it gave Henry VIII the excuse he was looking for to close down all the abbeys.

Many original features remain, including the glorious west front complete with an elaborate, richly carved doorway, beautiful rose window and fourteenth century inscription 'Abbot Adams carried out this work; may he rest in peace. Amen'.

MONTGOMERY CASTLE

Powys

The medieval chronicler Mathew Paris tells us that in 1223 Henry III's guardian, Hubert de Burgh, took the boy-king on a progress. When they arrived at Montgomery, Hubert showed him 'a suitable spot for the erection of an impregnable castle.' It was a perfect site. The road route from Shrewsbury to Montgomery, which is still followed by the modern road, was the obvious route for an English invasion of mid-Wales. Nearby there had been an iron age hillfort; there had also been an Anglo-Saxon stronghold and an early Norman castle, which had been abandoned as recently as 1216.

A spur of high ground ends dramatically in the castle rock, which gives a spectacular view of the low ground below. Hubert built his new castle there, which cost the boy-king more than £2,000. Once the royal castle was completed, it was granted to Hubert for life together with £130 for its upkeep. In 1229, Hubert was awarded a further £166 for 'enclosing' the castle. This entailed building an outer bailey wall. In 1233, Hubert roofed the tower with lead, and this seems to have marked the completion of the castle.

Montgomery was one of several royal castles held for the king by powerful subjects. It was risky, in that those powerful subjects could then use their state-of-the-art castles as power bases on their own account. Henry III was in fact later to quarrel with Hubert de Burgh, but during his minority the king had little choice but to entrust power to others. He nevertheless had a sound strategic sense, and became a great castle-builder in his own right. From Montgomery Castle, he learned that the best site for a fortress was on a high impregnable rock; failing that, water was the best defence. Henry's son Edward I inherited his sure sense of military strategy.

Montgomery Castle replaced the early Norman castles, but it too contained a great deal of timber. Remodelled by Edward I, Montgomery became one of the four royal border castles. The others were Chester, Shrewsbury and St Briavels. Later Montgomery was held by the Mortimers, and even then it was in a state of disrepair with only 'one lytle peece of waynscotte remayninge in the grett hall or dyning chamber. . . the wett putrifieth the timber.' Curiously, by the time of the Civil Wars, Montgomery was no longer considered a key location; there seems to have been no fighting there at all. The castle had dwindled to a ruin and the town to a village. But in Charles I's time, Sir Edward Herbert, who became Lord Herbert of Cherbury, built a new house in the castle grounds, and it was considered 'elegant and noble'. It stood for less than 30 years. After Lord Herbert's surrender to the Parliamentarians and subsequent death, both new and old castles were destroyed. Lord Herbert's son agreed to this, apparently hoping that the new castle, which he argued was unfortified, would be spared; both his home and his hopes fell in ruins.

The castle's remains, a few ravaged stumps of broken walling, give scant idea of the aspiring spirits of the Herbert family and their intensely civilized lifestyle.

ABERYSTWYTH CASTLE

CARDIGANSHIRE

Long before the Anglo-Norman kings of England began their castle-building programme in Wales, the strategic value of Aberystwyth was recognized. Iron Age settlers fortified Pen Dinas with one of the biggest hillforts in the region; that the fortification is well over 2,000 years old makes it all the more impressive.

With the Norman advance into Wales came the age of the stone castle. The first castle at Aberystwyth was nevertheless an earthen ringwork castle. This castle built by Gilbert de Clare was the scene of a great deal of intrigue, as Anglo-Normans and Welsh fought for control of the site.

Inevitably, the earth and timber fort built fairly low down was inadequate and a new site for a more permanent castle in stone was found. This time, it was the Welsh, led by Llewellyn the Great, who built the castle, and in a high, commanding, coastal location.

In the mid-thirteenth century Henry III tried to appease the Welsh by naming Llewellyn ap Gruffydd as Prince of Wales, but on the accession of Edward I, Llewellyn refused to pay homage to the new English king. By 1276, Edward tired of waiting and organized his first campaign against the Welsh. The following year, he ordered the construction of a series of strongholds in Wales, at points from which English control of the Welsh could be maintained. They included Rhuddlan and Aberystwyth, which were designed as concentric fortresses, rings of defences, walls within walls. In its day Aberystwyth Castle was as powerful as Conwy or Harlech.

This Edwardian castle once ranked among the greatest in Wales. Now it is a forlorn ruin, little more than a jumble of weathered masonry, indistinguishable from the natural sea-stacks and stumps to be found along any rocky coastline. Given the excellent state of the northern Welsh castles, the very poor state of Aberystwyth needs explaining. Its deterioration started as early as the fourteenth century. By 1343, when the Black Prince was in charge, several parts of the castle were already falling down, including the hall, the kitchen range and the main gateway. The location so close to the open sea, exposed to the pounding of high-energy waves, explains the rapidity of the disintegration.

Owen Glendower seized the castle in 1404, then the English seized it back. But after 1408 Aberystwyth lost its strategic value to the English kings and they stopped spending money on repairs. In 1649, the castle fell victim to Cromwell's uncompromising policy of slighting castles whose garrisons had sided with the King. After that, the castle became little more than a stone quarry for local builders.

There are, even so, enough elements surviving for the original design to be read. When complete, the diamond-shaped plan included two twin-towered gate-houses, a barbican gate and four gateways. Now, there is a gorsedd circle of stones raised for a modern-day Eisteddfod, an unjustifiable addition. Overall, the felled stumps of Aberystwyth Castle are disturbing rather than picturesque. They have been described as 'the tottering remains of a once magnificent and formidable building.'

BRECON CATHEDRAL

BRECKNOCKSHIRE

Brecon Cathedral stands on high ground above the Honddu River in the northern part of the town of Brecon. After the Norman conquest of England in 1066, there was an uneasy truce between the Welsh chieftains and the Norman invaders. This began to disintegrate as Norman lords broke free of royal control and started occupying territory on the Welsh borders. One of these Norman lords was Bernard of Neufmarche. His activities in the area culminated in a battle near Brecon in 1093; the local Welsh chieftain was killed and Bernard built himself a castle at Brecon to control the area. He also gave an existing church, dedicated to St John the Evangelist, and standing close to the castle, to a monk called Roger from Battle Abbey in Sussex. Roger arrived with other Benedictine monks to set up a priory on the site.

Brecon Priory was formally founded as a daughter house of Battle Abbey. With support from Battle and the patronage of successive Lords of Brecon, Brecon Priory gradually grew from its foundation in 1100 until the Dissolution of the monasteries in 1537.

Brecon Cathedral and the ancillary monastic buildings round it date from various times right through this period and beyond. Some parts of the cathedral survive from the beginning of the Norman period, then the building was enormously enlarged in Early English style in the thirteenth century; it was added to again in the fourteenth century in decorated style.

In the later middle ages, Brecon Cathedral became an important place of pilgrimage. This development followed the installation of a Golden Rood on the screen at the eastern end of the nave. It was common for a screen of wood or stone to separate the nave from the chancel, and for this screen to be decorated with images of saints. This particular one had a gilded Crucifix suspended above it, which was a wonder in itself, and sufficient reason to travel to see it. It gave the church its second name, the Church of the Holy Rood.

The south transept was once known as Capel Cochiaid, the Chapel of the Red-Haired Men, possibly after the garrison of Norman soldiers who may have used it as a burial place. The chancel vault, designed by Gilbert Scott, conceals two older roofs above it, from the seventeenth and fifteenth centuries.

There were never very many monks at Brecon, but they were evidently dedicated to learning and teaching. Several books written at Brecon had survived and replicas are on show.

The Priory was shut down in 1537 and the property passed into secular hands, specifically the hands of Sir John Price. The church survived as a parish church for the town. Some of the chapels fell into ruin, but the nave and tower continued in use. In the 1860s, the building was restored by Sir Gilbert Scott, who recreated it as a fine, plain, massive and rather squat structure. The low square tower has more the feeling of a medieval castle gate-house. Even so, the overall impression is of great strength and solidity. When the Church of Wales was disestablished in 1920, the Priory Church became the Cathedral Church of a new diocese, Swansea and Brecon.

CAREW CASTLE

PEMBROKESHIRE

In 1100 Arnulph de Montgomery, who had opposed Henry I, found himself deprived by the King of his possessions in Pembrokeshire. They included Pembroke Castle, which was given to Gerald Fitzwalter of Windsor, Arnulph's castellan. Shortly afterwards, Gerald Fitzwalter started building himself a new home at Carew. Gerald's eldest son, William, adopted the local place-name as his surname, following English usage, becoming de Carew.

The most famous of the Carews was Sir Nicholas de Carew, who distinguished himself in Ireland and in putting down a local Pembrokeshire rebellion. In 1300 he joined the Earl of Pembroke in accompanying Edward I into Scotland and was present at the siege of Caerlaverock.

In 1480, Carew Castle passed to Sir Rhys ap Thomas, the richest man in Wales. He backed the cause of Henry Richmond, which decided the outcome of the Wars of the Roses. Richmond, as Henry VII, did not forget Sir Rhys, making him a Garter Knight and in 1507, to celebrate his admission to the Garter, Sir Rhys held a five-day tournament at Carew Castle, including Mass, plays, feasting, wrestling, throwing the bar, tilting at the quintain, tossing the pike and hunting, as well as the jousting. It was the last great tournament ever to be held in Britain. The thing that was remembered about the event long afterwards was the remarkably high standard of behaviour at the tournament. Although a thousand men spent five days together, there was not one quarrel, not one unkind word, not so much as a hostile glance.

But the dark poison of politics worked on in the background. Sir Rhys's grandson, who inherited Carew Castle, was executed on Tower Hill for treason in 1531. Shortly after this, in the reign of Elizabeth I, Sir John Perrot applied for the Lordship of Carew and was given it, but he too was sentenced to death for treason in 1591. The castle passed to Robert, Earl of Essex, and into other hands again. Carew Castle does not seem to have brought its owners much luck.

Carew Castle started off as a timber Norman motte and bailey castle. By 1200 it had been replaced in stone. The major part of the surviving castle dates from the thirteenth century. By 1250, it consisted of a single strong square enclosure with drum-shaped towers at its corners; these enable the defenders to give some flanking fire along the walls. The east front dates from 1270. The south wall was bombarded and broken open by Parliamentarian troops. The west front, also dating from 1270, has great medieval dignity and strength; this was thoroughly reconstructed in the reign of Henry VII by Sir Rhys. Within the west wall was the huge Great Hall, which Sir Rhys also rebuilt.

But what most people notice and remember of this very fine ruin is the north front, with its great stone mullioned windows looking out over the Carew River. The work of Sir John Perrot, this is a magnificent example of Elizabethan architecture.

CILGERRAN CASTLE

PEMBROKESHIRE

Cilgerran Castle has one of the finest situations of all the castles in south-west Wales. It stands on the south bank of the River Teifi and is defended on two sides by steep cliffs. When it was built is disputed by historians. Some say it was built by Gerald de Windsor, the castellan of Pembroke Castle, between 1110 and 1115. Others say it was the great Roger de Montgomery, commander of the right flank of the Norman army at Hastings, who started building the castle in 1092.

Whichever Norman or Anglo-Norman builder was responsible, Cilgerran Castle like all the other Norman castles in Wales became a focus for the hatred of the local Welsh people. They attacked this symbol of oppression and conquest repeatedly and the Normans sustained heavy losses. In 1169, Gilbert de Clare, Earl of Pembroke, completed the building of Cilgerran Castle, probably adding the stone curtain wall at this time.

Shortly after this, the great Welsh leader Lord Rhys ap Gruffydd attacked and seized the castle, imprisoning the Norman castellan, Robert FitzStephen. Some months later, an Anglo-Norman force together with a detachment of Flemings who had settled in the area made an attempt to regain Cilgerran. They failed. Lord Rhys was there to stay. Cilgerran became his principal stronghold. In 1172, Henry II stopped at Cilgerran en route for Ireland and was entertained at the castle by Lord Rhys.

The Welsh occupation of a Norman stronghold was an anomaly that could not be allowed to continue indefinitely, though, and in 1204 William Marshall, Earl of Pembroke, marched on Cilgerran Castle with a huge army. His determined attack put the Welsh occupants to flight and he was able to hold the castle for a further ten years before Llewellyn ap Iorwerth retook it.

Thirteenth century Cilgerran had inner and outer baileys, five gates and a gatehouse with portcullis and stout round towers. The walls were very thick and built of thin slate-like stones. Although it withstood a fierce onslaught in 1258, by 1275 the castle had become neglected. A report noted, 'We found the castle defective in towers and in all other buildings.' The report included an estimate for the cost of repairs.

John Leland does not refer to Cilgerran at all, which may mean that the castle was of no importance in the sixteenth century, but we do know that the place was garrisoned by Royalists in the Civil War and given a pounding by Parliamentarian guns. Several cannon balls from this episode have been found round the castle. The usual period of neglect followed. Eventually, in 1929, the castle was rented to the Cilgerran Town Trust in a poor state with a view to its renovation. In 1938, Mrs Colby bought Cilgerran Castle and gave it to the National Trust. It now consists of two courtyards or baileys and two towers, to south-east and south-west, which were once known as the Red and White Towers. There are also remnants of curtain walls, a chapel and a gatehouse.

124

MANORBIER CASTLE

PEMBROKESHIRE

Manorbier Castle is a graceful and elegant ruin, hiding in a valley near the sea. It has the distinction of being the only castle in Wales that was never attacked, never besieged. It skulks like a guerrilla in its hideaway, with a view of the sea yet invisible from the sea. It was probably overlooked by predatory coastal raiders.

Manorbier Castle was founded by Odo de Barri, who was one of the followers of Gerald de Windsor, castellan of the main Norman fortress of Pembroke. Gerald had set up his personal stronghold and home at Carew, a few kilometres from Manorbier. Odo's son married Gerald's daughter Angharad, and their numerous offspring became a very important Pembrokeshire family. Two of Angharad's sons, Philip and Robert, became soldiers, the third became a priest and achieved lasting fame travelling and writing, under the name Gerald of Wales. Part-English, part-Welsh, he was despised by both Welsh and English.

Henry IV took the castle away from the de Barri family in 1399. The castle passed from one owner to another over the next 200 years. By the time John Leland saw it in the 1530s it was unoccupied and ruined. In the Civil War, Manorbier was occupied by Parliamentary forces, but it was not involved in any siege.

Odo's original stronghold was a motte and bailey, but nothing of that phase has survived. The castle is a single rectangular ward (enclosure) with no keep. It has instead a strongly built gatehouse and a well preserved drum tower embedded in the walls. The buildings within the ruined outer walls belong to the time of Henry II and Henry III, and include a lofty hall with a vaulted cellar.

Manorbier Castle was Gerald of Wales's birthplace, the place he loved best. This is how he described it in about 1180;

'The castle called Maenor Pyrr is excellently well defended by turrets and bulwarks, having on its northern and southern sides a fish pond under its walls, as conspicuous for its grand appearance as for the depth of its waters, and a beautiful orchard, enclosed by a vineyard and a wood. . . Towards the west the Severn Sea, bending its course to Ireland, enters a hollow bay at some distance from the castle. From this point of sight, you will see almost all the ships from Great Britain, which the east wind drives upon the Irish coast, daringly brave the inconstant waves and raging sea. The country is well supplied with corn, sea-fish and imported wines, and it is tempered by a salubrious air. Demetia is the most beautiful as well as the most powerful district of Wales. . . Maenor Pyrr is the pleasantest spot in Wales.'

Manorbier Castle is a fine example of an early medieval baron's residence. Remarkably, all the facilities that made Manorbier such a pleasant home can still be traced – the church, mill, dovecote, pond, park and wood – very much as Gerald of Wales described eight centuries ago.

NARBERTH CASTLE

PEMBROKESHIRE

This desolate place was called Narberth a thousand years ago – before the Normans or the English arrived. The original old mound castle was raised about 3km (1.8 miles) to the south, where its round earthen motte can still be seen; it is known as Sentence Castle. According to Welsh legend, Sentence Castle was an important stronghold, but its position laid it wide open to attack, which is probably why the Normans gave it up in the mid-thirteenth century. Instead they built a stone castle at Narberth. Sentence Castle was attacked and destroyed by Gruffydd, son of Rhys ap Tewdwr, in 1113 and again in 1116; it was attacked again in 1215 by Maelgwn ap Rhys.

The new castle at Narberth was a small but imposing and strong castle, built on a natural mound just south of the town. It was rectangular in shape with round towers at each corner. It seems there was no keep. Instead a residential range was built on one side of the quadrangle, facing the entrance.

There is one round tower that is in fair condition and standing up to three storeys high, but the rest of the castle is in a very bad state. Narberth Castle was rebuilt more than once. Sir Andrew Perrott built the stone castle in 1346, but ten years later Llewellyn ap Gruffydd, the last native Prince of Wales, attacked and destroyed it. In the reign of Edward III the castle was rebuilt again. Records show that in Narberth there was an 'Englishry' and a 'Welshry'; in other words two distinct communities were living in the area. It is what we should expect in South Wales at this time of English colonization in what was seen as 'Little England'.

An inventory of furniture for Narberth Castle in 1330 tells us that it was equipped with two dining tables, three tables, seven benches, one tub, one tin, two old coffers, one ladder, one cask for butter, two empty casks and so on. The quantities are surprisingly small. What manner of castle had three casks, two crossbows and only one ladder?

The castle passed to the Crown in the reign of Edward III; Richard III sold it to Gruffydd ap Nicholas; Henry VIII granted it to Sir Rhys ap Thomas, who made great efforts to renovate and beautify it. Narberth was described in 1527 by John Leland as 'a little pretty pile of old Sir Rhys'.

In 1647 Narberth became one of the many castles to be bombarded by the Parliamentarian army, but after the Civil War it was still habitable. In 1677 a man called Captain Richard Castell, who set up large monthly cattle fairs and weekly markets at Narberth, was living there, though he is the last known resident. After Captain Castell's death the castle fell increasingly into ruin. An engraving of 1740 shows that walls, arched doorways and windows still survived, along with a gable end, some chimneys and a complete gateway. But today, Narberth Castle is a complete ruin – and looking like little more than a collection of eroded sea-stacks.

PEMBROKE CASTLE

PEMBROKESHIRE

Pembroke Castle is a magnificent castle in a magnificent setting. It occupies a strong defensive position on a rocky hill, surrounded on three sides by a tidal river. Arnulph de Montgomery, the Norman conqueror of Pembrokeshire and son of Roger de Montgomery, built his first fortress in the region at Pembroke in 1090. It was at first built of turf and timber, but effectively resisted attacks from the Welsh. Cadwgan ap Bleddyn tried to take it in 1092 but without success. This simple motte and bailey castle became the inner ward of the imposing stone castle that we now see.

When Arnulph returned to England, the stronghold was held by Gerald de Windsor, who was half-Norman, half-Saxon. Gerald was a brilliant castellan, who held Pembroke against a series of assaults by Welsh rebels by a combination of bravery, cunning and obstinacy. When Henry I was betrayed by Arnulph, he handed Pembroke Castle over to Gerald. It was probably Gerald who replaced the wooden palisade surrounding the inner ward with a stone wall. Gerald gradually turned Pembroke Castle into the first stone castle in Wales and the focal stronghold of 'Little England beyond Wales'.

When the earldom of Pembroke was created in 1138, Gilbert de Clare took the castle. It was Gilbert or his son Richard, known as Strongbow, who built the splendid circular Norman keep in the inner ward. It is 23m (75ft) high and the finest drum keep in Britain. William Marshal held the earldom from 1189 to 1219. The great Norman Earls of Pembroke – the de Clares, the Marshals, the de Valences, the Hastings – were very powerful magnates, powerful enough to risk defying the kings of England several times. One of the most powerful of all was the great Earl William, Marshal of England. In 1211 he entertained King John at Pembroke Castle; the King had 'come to Pembroke to cross to Ireland'. After William Marshal died in 1219, the Welsh under Llewellyn ap Iorwerth rose in rebellion. Other castles fell to the Welsh, but not Pembroke.

William de Valence became Earl of Pembroke in 1265. He added bastions and three gates to Pembroke's town walls. He also made great changes to the castle, defending the roughly hexagonal outer ward with six towers, one at each angle. He added a fine and impressive gatehouse, which had three portcullises. Henry VII was born in one of the rooms in the gatehouse in January 1457, which is why it is now known as the Henry VII Tower. Pembroke Castle was Henry's boyhood home for 14 years. William de Valence experimented with a completely new feature, a battlemented flying arch which joined two round towers inside the outer ward. It is not clear what this was for.

In 1400 the Welsh rose against the English again, this time under the inspired leadership of Owain Glendower. The Governor of Pembroke Castle was Sir Francis A'Court, who arranged for the payment of a danegeld to Owain Glendower, who in turn left Pembroke Castle alone.

This was odd, because Pembroke was a very strong castle and could almost certainly have withstood Glendower's attack. One historian has called Pembroke 'the virgin fortress'; although the Welsh attacked and captured many other strongholds, such as Conwy and Harlech, Pembroke Castle was never taken.

In 1485, Jasper Tudor and his nephew Henry Richmond landed in Pembrokeshire; together with a force thousands strong and the support of Sir Rhys ap Thomas of Carew Castle, they marched to Bosworth, where they defeated and killed Richard III. Richmond became Henry VII by usurpation. His son Henry VIII gave Pembroke to Anne Boleyn. Pembroke was still in its hey-day, still a great working castle. In 1603 it was still a formidable fortress with 'all the walls standing strong, without any decay.'

In 1642, at the start of the Civil War, Pembroke declared for Parliament, while the rest of the Principality declared for the King. In 1644, Royalist forces laid siege to Pembroke Castle, but the defenders were able to hold out until a Parliamentary fleet sailed into Milford Haven, lifting the siege. The castle stayed in Parliamentary hands until the 'First' Civil War was won. Major General Laugharne, who was then in possession of the castle, was ordered by Cromwell to dismiss his men. Laugharne refused and was imprisoned. The Mayor of Pembroke, John Poyer, garrisoned the castle himself and declared for the King. He was declared a traitor by parliament. Cromwell himself arrived with a huge army in May 1648 and laid siege to Pembroke Castle, setting fire to parts of the town. Poyer and Laugharne surrendered on 11 July. Their gentlemen-officers were allowed to go free but ordered to leave the country within six weeks. A military court condemned Laugharne, Poyer and Colonel Powell to death, but the

Council of State decided that the death of one man would 'satisfy the ends of justice'. The three men drew lots and Poyer was executed at Covent Garden in London.

Then, with a sad inevitability, Cromwell sentenced Pembroke Castle to death too. He ordered its slighting. The barbican gate and five towers of the outer ward were blown up, together with the curtain wall of the inner ward. The ruins seem to have remained derelict until 1880, when Mr J. R. Cobb of Brecon launched a three-year programme of partial restoration. Then there was a further period of neglect. In 1928 Pembroke Castle was acquired by Major General Sir Ivor Philipps. He had all the ivy stripped from the castle walls, he had the trees and shrubs rooted out, and he undertook major restoration work. When the General died in 1959 his daughter leased the castle to Pembroke Borough Council, who took on the responsibility for conserving it.

Pembroke Castle is one of the finest castles in these islands. But is also has an curious secret. Under the keep is a natural cavern about 24m (80ft) across, called the Wogan. It was entered by a staircase half in the rock, half in a turret. Leland said, 'In the botom of the great stronge tower in the inner ward is a marvelus vault caullid the Hogan'.

Pembroke has one of the largest castles in Wales. However, despite its size and appearance it was not a royal castle but the possesion of a private lord - his residence and the administrative centre of his territories. Pembroke Castle occupies a strong position high on a ridge between two tidal inlets. Its fortifications were continually extended throughout its history and it displays stonework from many periods.

ST DAVID'S CATHEDRAL

PEMBROKESHIRE

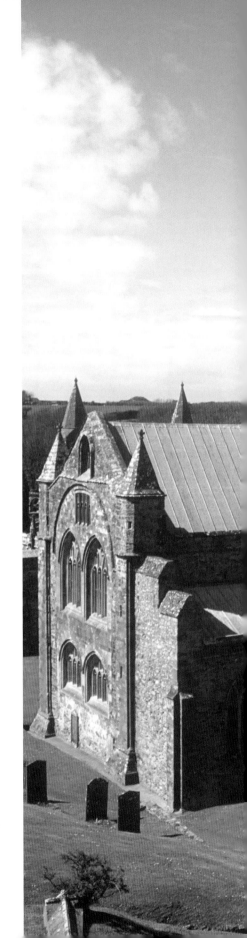

The cathedral city of St David's is no more than a straggling village on a treeless windswept plateau. It is the smallest cathedral city in Britain, and yet it is incredibly ancient, having been the seat of a bishop since the sixth century. But St David's Cathedral is not just for St David's, it is for the whole of Pembrokeshire – south-west Wales is its sea-surrounded see. St David's Cathedral nestles on the sheltered floor of the deep wooded Alun valley below the 'city'. The Alun valley is also known as Glyn Rhosyn, the Valley of the Small Bog.

The cathedral is imposing – the largest and finest in Wales – but also a rather strange-looking building, with a tall and massive square tower and a low nave and chancel with almost flat roofs dating from 1530–40; clearly the building would look far better if the nave and chancel were fitted with steeply pitched roofs to match those on the transepts. The cathedral close still has its long boundary wall and one of its gate-houses: originally there were four. The visitor approaches the cathedral up a flight of 39 steps, known as 'The Thirty-Nine Articles'.

The building we now see was begun in 1181, and it replaces at least three earlier churches on the same site, which is the spot where St David himself founded a monastic settlement in the sixth century, transferring his community from Whitesand Bay in 550, but nothing of this early settlement now survives. St David died in 589.

Because of its historic associations with the patron saint of Wales, St David's has been a pilgrimage focus for fourteen centuries. In 1123, Bishop Bernard secured a 'privilege' from Pope Calixtus II to turn St David's into a centre for pilgrimage. The Pope obligingly declared that two pilgrimages to St David's were equal to one to Rome; three were equal to a journey to Jerusalem. It was also a great centre of learning. In the ninth century, King Alfred asked for help from St David's in rebuilding the intellectual life of Wessex. But St David's had problems of its own. In 1080, Bishop Abraham was killed by the Danes. In 1089, David's shrine was vandalized and stripped of the gold and silver decoration.

But the high status of St David's was never doubted. In 1171, shortly after the murder of Thomas Becket, Henry II visited St David's and the present cathedral building was begun. The 'new' tower fell down in 1220, smashing the choir and transepts, and there was further damage to the cathedral in an earthquake in 1247.

At the time of the Reformation, Bishop Barlow stripped David's shrine of its jewels and confiscated the saint's relics to counteract 'superstition'. In 1648, the building was destroyed by Parliamentary soldiers.

Then came the restorations. Nash rebuilt the west front in 1793. Sir George Scott undertook restoration work 1862–77, and the Lady Chapel was restored in 1901. It is a great pity Scott did not have the nerve to raise the roofs of the nave and chancel, which would have turned St David's Cathedral into a great building.

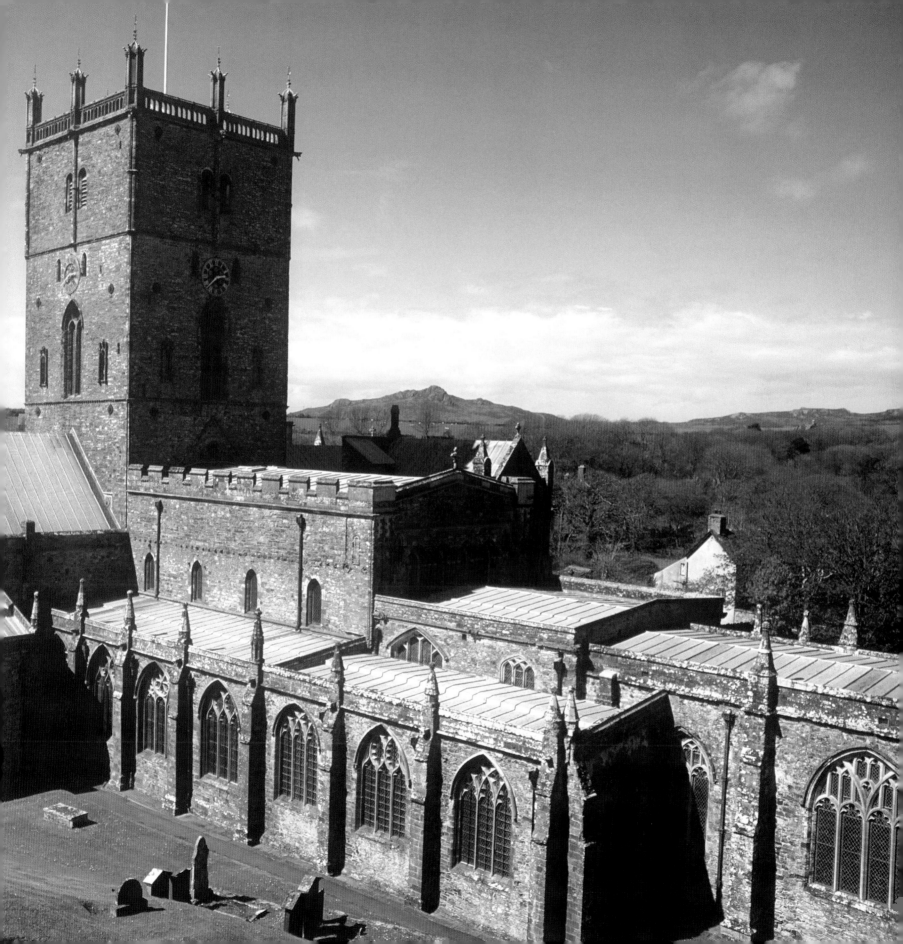

CALDICOT CASTLE

aldicot Castle stands on a site that had been recognized for its strategic value long before the castle itself was built. The Romans actively made use of the area, which stood on the Via Julia to Caerwent, the Roman town of Venta Silurum just to the north. Caldicot's position close to the Bristol Channel meant that it was a good vantage point from which to watch the comings and goings of ships; it was also an easy place to provision by water.

The Normans recognized the usefulness of Caldicot as early as 1086. They built a motte, two baileys and a deep surrounding ditch, and used the strong-point to control this area of South Wales. The Norman motte, a well-made grass-covered round mound, is still a conspicuous feature of the site. Originally it supported a timber tower. This was replaced by a round stone keep in 1221, after Humphrey de Bohun, the 'Good Earl' of Hereford, inherited the lordship of Caldicot. The de Bohuns held the lordship by inheritance until 1373, after which it became the property of the Crown.

The four-storeyed keep with its local gritstone walls 3m (10ft) thick, was a very strong structure that could withstand any assault imaginable in the early middle ages. The lowest storey of the keep was buried inside the motte, for structural stability, and the main entry point into the keep was by way of a staircase up the motte. It was in fact quite common for even free-standing keeps to have their entrances well above ground level.

Inside the keep, the architecture was refined

and elaborate and the accommodation was luxurious. Spiral staircases allowed people to move easily from floor to floor, there were fireplaces with hoods to remove the smoke, there were window-seats. There was also a latrine-turret. A vaulted dungeon in the basement was reached by way of a trapdoor in its ceiling. The outside of the keep at Caldicot was, and still is, faced with finely-cut smooth ashlar stonework, and buttressed at its base with a splayed (or 'battered') plinth.

The roofline of the keep was originally crowned with battlements, and put-log holes in the walls show where timbers once supported a wooden walkway along the battlements. Arrow slits perforate the walls, improving the keep's defences.

Today the keep is non-combatant, an obsolete reminder of a time when warfare was simple, crude, low-tech. The tourist's climb to the top of the keep gives a wonderful view of the surrounding beautifully wooded countryside. It also gives an excellent idea of the layout of the castle.

The next phase of building at Caldicot came as soon as the keep was finished, and it set the seal on the rest of the design. Running down the motte from the walls of the keep were stout curtain walls that went out and round the inner ward; these walls were strengthened with round corner towers. The towers at the south-west and south-east angles were massive, and only slightly smaller than the keep.

In the thirteenth century the castle's first gate-house was installed, halfway between the keep and the south-west tower. This was a simple doorway piercing yet another round tower; it still stands to almost its full original height. It was defended by a heavy wooden gate, a portcullis and murder holes.

In the fourteenth century a timber Great Hall was added along the inside of the curtain wall; only a few decorative windows in the curtain wall remain of this structure.

In 1373, the last male de Bohun died and the castle passed to two daughters, Eleanor and Mary. Mary married the future Henry IV. Eleanor married Thomas of Woodstock, Duke of Gloucester, and it was he who took over Caldicot, launching an expensive building programme. He added the three-storeyed Woodstock Tower, installing a bath – a very rare refinement in medieval castles.

Thomas Woodstock's enjoyment of Caldicot was brief. He was murdered in Calais and the castle passed to his daughter Anne. The Duke of Gloucester's greatest contribution to Caldicot was the great gatehouse, which has now been restored to its original state on the south side of the castle. This had a drawbridge, two portcullises, two heavy timber gates, and three murder holes. Upstairs there was a lavish apartment suite. The twin turrets are decorated with unusual sculpted portrait heads; one is believed to represent Edward II. The residential focal point had shifted from the keep to the main gatehouse. This was the developmental trend of the middle ages; much the same process can be seen at Warwick Castle, where the keep waned into almost symbolic importance as a centrepiece, while the towers in the curtain wall became a hive of activity.

Anne Woodstock married Edmund Earl of Stratford. Their son, Humphrey, kept the castle and became the first Duke of Buckingham. When Buckingham died during the Wars of the Roses, Caldicot Castle became Crown property and was passed to the Dukes of Stafford. Edward, the third Duke, was distrusted by Henry VIII and in 1521 he was beheaded for treason. Henry VIII then granted Caldicot to the Dukes of Lancaster, who let the property to a sequence of tenants.

The antiquary, J. R. Cobb, bought Caldicot Castle in 1855 and set about restoring it to its medieval state. Cobb was passionate about castles, and he was personally responsible for rescuing three Welsh castles. The other two were Manorbier and Pembroke. As at Manorbier, Cobb made Caldicot Castle his home while he worked on it, devoting a huge amount of energy to restoring the structure. He did a good job, producing an appropriate mix of the genuinely old and the carefully and authentically restored. He left most of the original stonework intact.

Caldicot Castle is now owned and operated by the local authority, and is open to the public. It is a surprising discovery – a very fine and beautiful castle that has not been strangled by its own popularity and success as a tourist attraction.

RAGLAN CASTLE

MONMOUTHSHIRE

Raglan Castle is one of the most picturesque and romantic ruined castles. The first castle to be built at Raglan was a Norman motte and bailey castle. This survived until early in the fifteenth century, when Raglan came into the possession of Sir William ap Thomas.

Sir William was a Welsh knight who had fought at the Battle of Agincourt with Henry V in 1415, and like others doubtless returned with a self-image bursting with patriotic valour and chivalry; like other such veterans, he wanted a home that matched his self-image. In 1435 he started building the Great Tower, which is the oldest surviving part of the castle. This was a significant departure from the Norman concept of a keep, which was normally square or round in plan. Sir William's keep was unusual in being hexagonal in plan and surrounded by its own moat.

Originally the Great Tower was accessible only by a drawbridge from the main body of the castle; this has been replaced by a fixed bridge. It is said that the unusual defences of the keep reflect the owner's suspicious nature, enabling him to isolate himself from his own household in the event of a shift in their loyalties. It seems more likely that it was a defensive work more in the spirit of the fortress-within-fortress wards and baileys of other castles.

Lord Herbert, the son of the first Marquess of Worcester, installed an unusual contraption in the tower which frightened some commissioners who arrived to search the castle for arms. A hydraulic engine roared into life to raise a large quantity of water up to the battlements and pour it through the machicolations onto the heads of the intruders. The roaring sound echoing round inside the tower was quite enough to frighten the commissioners off.

The hexagonal shape of the Yellow Tower of Gwent was a way of reducing the vulnerability of the right-angled corners of the square keep, yet removing the extra difficulty (and cost) of making a curved wall. It was ingenious, yet it was not an experiment that was widely repeated elsewhere. The cream-coloured stone of which the Great Tower was built gave it its nickname; it became known as the Yellow Tower of Gwent, which makes it sound like a location from a legend about King Arthur.

Sir William ap Thomas's son, William Herbert, Earl of Pembroke, continued the work of developing Raglan Castle, turning it into a high-medieval masterpiece. He added a great gatehouse and some lavish accommodation. The last important phase of building on the site was seen through in the middle of the sixteenth century by William Somerset, Earl of Worcester. He made improvements to the Great Hall of the castle. Even in its ruined state the hall is impressive. A large oriel window, once filled with heraldic stained glass, lit the high table, and the hall was heated in winter by a huge fireplace. The roof was supported by hammerbeams of Irish oak. Coats of arms and rich panelling covered the walls, and there was a minstrels' gallery above the screens passage at the lower end. It is easy to imagine Sir Walter Herbert entertaining Henry VII's queen, Elizabeth of York, here in 1502; her retinue included her own band, 'the Quenes mynstrelles'. Her husband, the King, knew Raglan well, as he had been sent there as a boy; it was customary for aristocratic boys to be farmed out to the households of other aristocrats, presumably to learn manners and independence.

The main stone used in the construction of Raglan Castle is sandstone, but of two different types. The fifteenth century castle is characterized by pale, almost yellowish sandstone from Redbrook on the Wye river, 5 km (3 miles) away. The other sandstone is local Old Red Sandstone, red, brown or purplish in colour, which was used in the Tudor work. A paler stone was also used in the making of the fireplaces. As you approach the gatehouse, the castle's yellow sandstone becomes obvious.

In the English Civil War, Raglan Castle was held by Royalists, and paid the inevitable price. Even if Raglan might have looked more like a fortified mansion than a castle, it was given 'enemy castle' treatment when, in June 1646, it came under attack from a Parliamentarian army three and a half thousand strong under Colonel Morgan. Raglan's misfortune was that it had been made the local Royalist headquarters. The Earl of Worcester, reputed to be the richest man in England, contributed vast sums to the Royalist cause; it was said that he kept all his money in the Great Tower. He entertained Charles I at Raglan on such a lavish scale that the King feared his visit would do more damage to the Royalist resources than an enemy siege.

After a heavy bombardment that went on for several weeks, the castle eventually surrendered, in August 1646, to Sir Thomas Fairfax, the commanding officer of the New Model Army. He had come in person to oversee the siege of Raglan. It was one of the longest sieges of the Civil War, a tribute to the castle's strength, and Raglan Castle was among the last of the Royalist strongholds to fall to Cromwell. The victorious Parliamentarians slighted the castle, but only with difficulty. They had had difficulty in taking Raglan Castle; now they had difficulty in knocking it down. After a major effort, they succeeded in knocking down two sides of the Great Tower by undermining them.

Sadly, they burned the Earl's library, with its irreplaceable collection of old Welsh manuscripts. They also imprisoned the octogenarian Earl, promising him that he would be buried at Windsor. He replied, 'God bless my soul, they will give me a grander castle when dead than they took from me when living!' He did in fact die soon afterwards, and was buried in St George's Chapel, Windsor.

As elsewhere, further damage was done later by pilfering, which continued into the eighteenth century. The Duke of Beaufort ransacked Raglan for fittings for his new home at Badminton. The fifth Duke called a halt to the damage and from that moment on the castle was preserved as a tourist attraction. The ruined shell of Raglan Castle is still a very fine and impressive building. As you approach its main gateway, it gives the impression of being complete. Many of the walls stand to their full height and the fine machicolations along the tower tops give it a distinctively finished and ready-for-action look. Only the window holes, like the eyeless sockets of a skeleton, speak of its ruination. Raglan is like Bodiam Castle in Sussex, in being no more than an empty shell, yet a near-complete shell for all that, and still retaining the shape and majesty of the high medieval castle in all its glory.

SKENFRITH CASTLE

MONMOUTHSHIRE

Skenfrith Castle was one of three castles built within a few kilometres to guard the routes in and out of Wales between the Black Mountains and the River Wye. The Three Castles, sometimes known as the Trilateral Castles, were Skenfrith, White and Grosmont. To begin with they were made of timber; Skenfrith was later rebuilt in sandstone.

In the late 1130s, King Stephen brought the Three Castles together under a single Lordship so that the three fortresses could be controlled in a co-ordinated way as a single defensive unit. In the early thirteenth century Hubert de Burgh, Earl of Kent and Justiciar of England, held the Lordship of the Three Castles. He built modern stone castles at Grosmont and Skenfrith. At Grosmont the shape and size of the new castle was to a great extent controlled by the old mound on which it was to be built. At Skenfrith, Hubert de Burgh had the site levelled so that he could start from scratch.

Skenfrith Castle was built on low, level ground on the west bank of the River Monnow at Abergavenny. The curtain walls make a big irregular quadrilateral with round towers strengthening each corner. Inside there was the usual domestic range, which included a hall on the west side. In the middle of the enclosure stands a small drum-shaped keep on a low grassy mound; in its present shattered state it makes a very fine picturesque ruin.

The lower walls of the keep are 'battered', deliberately inward-sloping, to give the structure greater stability and strength. There is also a semi-circular projection from the keep wall; this contained a spiral staircase that connected the three storeys inside the keep. There was a basement and two upper storeys. After the round keep was built on the flat site, earth was heaped up round it, burying the lower storey and making it look as if the keep had been built on top of a motte. This was done at some other castles too, and it was probably to make sure that the keep walls were properly founded on solid ground.

The Lordship of the Three Castles was granted to Edmund Crouchback, Earl of Lancaster, in 1267. Although all three castles were owned and maintained by the Earls of Lancaster, only Grosmont Castle was used as a residence. The western range of the living quarters was below ground level when built, and must have been flooded by the Monnow every winter. Now unroofed, these chambers collect rainwater, and steps lead unpromisingly down into deep pools. It was understandable that the Lancasters chose Grosmont; consequently it was only Grosmont that saw any further development. As a result of this, Skenfrith Castle stayed much the same as when Hubert de Burgh finished it.

The great days of the Three Castles were in the conquest of Wales by Edward I of England. Once the conquest was accomplished, the Three Castles were not nearly so important. By the sixteenth century, all three of them, the favoured Grosmont included, were abandoned and falling into ruin.

CHEPSTOW CASTLE

Chepstow Castle was one of the first phase of Norman castles, built in the first five years after the Conquest in 1066. William I returned to Normandy immediately after his conquest of England, and Chepstow and the other first-wave castles were built at speed under the supervision of his viceroys, William FitzOsbern and Bishop Odo of Bayeux. It will have been FitzOsbern who oversaw the building of Chepstow.

The Normans set up their fortresses at Chepstow and Monmouth in preparation for the conquest of Wales. In 1093–4 they duly pushed on farther into South Wales from Chepstow, building new castles at Pembroke, Cardiff, Carmarthen and Cardigan. Although in this book we tend to look at each castle as having its own individual history, which it certainly has, it is sometimes useful to see that history within the context of a larger strategy. The Normans used their castles, from the first two that they built at Pevensey and Hastings on, as stepping stones in the conquest of England and Wales. Edward I, in a similar way later on, used his castles to throw a ring of stone round rebellious North Wales.

Chepstow Castle was built on a natural hill, a curving spur of sandstone overlooking a river crossing on the Wye. Chepstow also had a harbour, which meant that it could be supplied by water from Bristol. It was also possible to send troops or materials by water upriver or along the coast to the west. The several advantages of a coastal location, discovered by the Normans, were also later to be exploited when Edward I selected sites for his great castles in the north of Wales.

A substantial part of FitzOsbern's hall survives at Chepstow, along with the basic defences. They are even so only the nucleus of the massive castle built on the site by William the Marshall and later the Earls of Norfolk. Chepstow Castle saw further changes in the sixteenth and seventeenth centuries, but these were mostly minor alterations and embellishments.

Chepstow saw belated and rather futile action in the Civil War in the 1640s. Cromwell was angered by the 'mischievous' and unnecessary Second Civil War. The castles involved were commanded by officers who had broken their oaths and changed sides in order to defend the monarchy. Cromwell was directly involved in the field, and very aware of the hardship and bloodshed involved in storming these heavily defended fortresses. Chepstow was among a group of strong Welsh castles that put up significant resistance in this Second Civil War; the others were Tenby, Chirk and Pembroke. Chepstow was a castle of the Somersets, where Sir Nicholas Kemeys commanded a garrison of 120 men. Cromwell built a four-gun battery, knocked down the battlements to deprive the garrison of its artillery and then knocked down the curtain wall. After that the garrison ran off and Sir Nicholas himself was killed during the final assault.

In the nineteenth century the castle fell into neglect, lost its roof and was abandoned. Chepstow Castle as it now stands is a fine and substantial Gothic ruin, with weighty round towers, battlements and a fine sturdy gatehouse with twin round towers pressing in on a dark doorway.

TINTERN ABBEY

MONMOUTHSHIRE

Tintern is the best known of all the ruined abbeys in these islands. The surviving remains are substantial, they lie in a picturesque location beside the River Wye, and the visitor sees them against a backdrop of steep and densely wooded hillsides.Unlike Fountains, where there are distant glimpses, we come across Tintern Abbey suddenly and without warning. The north side does not catch the sun and the dark masonry is gaunt and forbidding. But Tintern is powerfully impressive and has been a focal monument for Romantic poets and painters from Wordsworth and Turner on. When they saw it, it was a different place. There was no road beside it then, and the ruin had not been tidied up by a succession of well-meaning heritage bodies. The litter of carved and sculpted fallen stones lying on hummocky ground has been cleared away and the land levelled. Then there was ivy; now there is mown grass. But there are always two views on conservation and presentation. There are those who want to smarten and restore a site like Tintern, which could easily be re-roofed, and there are those who want to see it let go into a more ruinous state still. The Revd William Gilpin once argued that a few well-aimed blows with a hammer would improve the picturesqueness of the too-well-preserved gable ends. At Tintern I can empathize with both of those views. It is not entirely satisfactory as it stands, neither restored nor a picturesque ruin.

Tintern Abbey was one of the first great Cistercian communities in Britain, founded in 1131 by Richard FitzRichard, the Lord of Chepstow, in a secluded spot in the densely wooded valley of the Wye. The monastery was founded just a year before Rievaulx to house a community of Cistercian monks from the monastery of L'Aumone in Normandy. As a Cistercian house, the same austerity might have been expected as at the sister house in Yorkshire, but the church was rebuilt in the thirteenth century as the original one was too small; by the thirteenth century Tintern was rich and ambitious and the stone carving – Early English and Decorated – had turned opulent.

Much of the twelfth century phase of the abbey has gone during the course of rebuilding in the thirteenth and fourteenth centuries, so quite a lot of the early architecture has gone. Most of Tintern's documented history has been lost too because its records were destroyed when Raglan Castle was ransacked in the Civil War. But we do know that when Richard I was taken prisoner, Tintern had to surrender its wool production for an entire year as its contribution towards the colossal £100,000 ransom. It is also known that soon after its expensive rebuilding,

The Cistercian abbey of Tintern is one of the greatest monastic ruins of Wales. It was only the second Cistercian foundation in Britain, and the first in Wales, and was founded on 9 May 1131 by Walter de Clare, Lord of Chepstow. It soon prospered, thanks to endowments of land in Gwent and Gloucestershire, and buildings were added and updated in every century until its dissolution in 1536.

Tintern played host to Edward II, who sheltered there for two nights before going on to his death at Berkeley Castle. In return for their hospitality, the doomed king granted the monks fishing rights on a stretch of the Wye.

Some time after this, the number of both monks and lay brothers at the monastery was drastically reduced, and that must have been because of the Black Death. The records are not there to prove it, but the reduction in staffing can only be explained in that way. Tintern may have been remote and isolated, but it cannot have escaped the effects of the Black Death, which is known to have swept through the valley of the River Severn in 1349, decimating the population as it passed.

Tintern Abbey's economy depended almost exclusively on agriculture, and probably made much of its money from the lucrative wool trade. This agricultural emphasis is underlined by the size of the lay brothers' refectory, which was significantly larger than that of the monks' refectory; medieval agriculture required a lot of human labour.

The abbey church is very well preserved, virtually complete apart from its roofs, window glass and tower. Its greatest feature is its great west window, consisting of seven lights, and its fine stone tracery is best appreciated from outside the precinct. The nave, which dates mainly from the thirteenth century, still has its clerestory on its south side. The lovely arches at the crossing once supported a square tower, and beyond that is the finely proportioned east window.

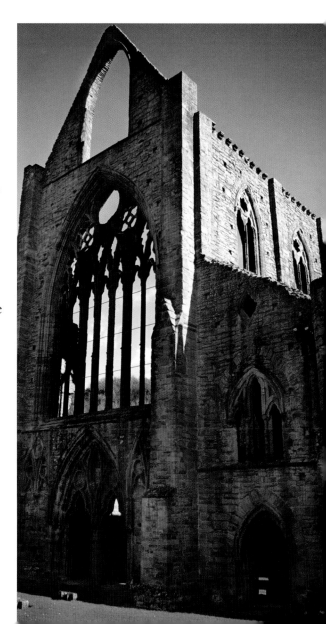

The constraints of the valley floor site led the architects to place the large complex of cloisters and other monastic buildings on the north side of the church. To the north-east, beyond the cloisters and the various rooms leading off it – library, chapter house, monks' frater – is yet another cloister garth, called the infirmary cloister. Beyond that again are the abbot's lodging and abbot's hall. Tintern Abbey made great use of the river as a waterway, and the adjacent hotel stands on the site of the abbey's watergate, where a thirteenth century arch provides access to a slipway.

When the Dissolution came in 1536, Abbot Richard Wyche surrendered Tintern to the King's commissioners. The site was granted to the Earl of Worcester, but only after the king's plumbers had been over it to strip the lead from the roof and take the bells from the tower above the crossing. The monastic buildings suffered far worse than the abbey church itself. It was a shameful exercise in asset-stripping, wrecking both an architectural masterpiece and a useful economic and humanitarian institution, and it was an exercise repeated again and again round the kingdom. After this episode, Tintern's fate was to sink into quiet obscurity. Its remoteness protected it to some extent from robbing for building stone, though there was some small-scale robbing of stone for use in local houses.

Gradually the woodland stole back across the abbey site, and the ivy grew unbidden, turning it into a classic Gothic ruined abbey, just in time for the great vogue in Romantic ruins in the late eighteenth and early nineteenth centuries. Tintern Abbey became one of the 'must-see' sites for the Romantics. Turner's beautiful watercolours of the ivy-grown crossing are still among the definitive images, not only of Tintern but of the Romantic movement.

CAERPHILLY CASTLE

GLAMORGAN

Caerphilly Castle is a veritable giant among castles; it is the biggest castle in Wales and one of the biggest castles in the whole of Britain and Ireland. It covers around 12 hectares (30 acres) of land, which means that only Windsor Castle is larger than Caerphilly. The poet Tennyson commented, 'It isn't a castle – it's a town in ruins.' He was right. Looked at across the water, Caerphilly Castle does look like a small walled medieval city.

The site was defended by the Roman army as early as AD 75, when auxiliaries from the Second Augusta Legion stationed at Caerleon built a fort. It stood beside one of the main Roman roads, halfway between the forts at Cardiff and Gelligaer. When the Romans gave the site up, it was left abandoned for a thousand years. And when the medieval castle was built, it was designed and built all in one go, from the ground up.

When the Normans arrived in South Wales, they initially controlled only the fertile coastal strip, leaving the hill country inland in the hands of the Welsh. By 1263, a large area in South Wales was in the hands of Gilbert de Clare, Earl of Gloucester and Hereford and Lord of Glamorgan, one of the most powerful of the Marcher lords, the lords of the Welsh border country. Gilbert, known as 'Red Gilbert' because of his red hair, was a very influential figure, who gave support to Simon de Montfort in his campaign to reduce the power of the King. When Llewellyn ap Gruffydd was rewarded for supporting de Montfort with the title Prince of Wales, which gave him sovereignty over Welsh barons, Gilbert changed sides, going over to Lord Edward, who would shortly become Edward I. After de Montfort was killed at the Battle of Evesham, his son and supporters fled to Kenilworth Castle, taking refuge there. Red Gilbert was among the Lord Edward's supporters who attacked them there. He was able to observe at close quarters the impressive system of defences that surrounded Kenilworth Castle, and in particular the elaborate water defences which included a massive artificial lake.

The site was chosen because of its strategic position in the communications system; it guarded the entrance to several valleys, as well as sitting close to the old Roman road route from Chepstow to Brecon. From Caerphilly it was possible to command a great deal of territory.

Work started on building Caerphilly Castle in 1268, when 'Red Gilbert' de Clare, the red-haired Lord of Glamorgan, became locked in a power struggle with Llewellyn ap Gruffydd, the Prince of Wales.

The design of this castle is a magnificent example of a medieval concentric plan; it is both the earliest and the best. A high and massive curtain wall surrounding the central inner ward is in turn surrounded by a lower and lighter outer curtain wall. That in turn is surrounded by extensive water defences, modelled on the water defences Gilbert had seen at Kenilworth. Caerphilly Castle was built in effect on three man-made islands; the large lakes round it were created by damming two streams. The curtain wall that flanks 300m (984ft) of the town's Castle Street is actually a dam, holding back the water of the two streams on each side of the castle.

Llewellyn saw this large-scale castle-building project as a direct challenge to his authority, as indeed it was, and in the autumn of 1270 he attacked and burnt the half-built structure. De Clare started rebuilding at once. But then Llewellyn rashly challenged the authority of the new king, Lord Edward who had now become King Edward I. After a major Welsh campaign, Edward succeeded in defeating and killing Llewellyn.

The castle was more or less complete in 1277; it impressed Edward to the extent that he went back to London to rebuild the Tower on a concentric plan with a moat.

After Llewellyn's removal, Caerphilly Castle became more of an administrative centre for the de Clare estates. After Gilbert de Clare's son was killed at the Battle of Bannockburn in 1314, there was no male heir and Caerphilly Castle came under royal control until the future of the estates could be decided. A Welsh rebellion in the area brought an attack in 1316 by Llewellyn Bren with 10,000 men. This attack failed and caused no damage to the castle. Llewellyn Bren was captured and thrown into the Tower of London.

In 1317, the de Clare estates were divided among Gilbert's three sisters. The eldest of these was married to Hugh Despenser, the favourite of Edward II. Despenser was greedy and unscrupulous, and tried to grab the rest of the de Clare estates from his brothers-in-law. In

Caerphilly Castle is one of the great medieval castles of western Europe. Several factors give it this pre-eminence - its immense size (covering approximately 30 acres), making it the largest in Britain after Windsor, its large-scale use of water for defence and the fact that it is the first truly concentric castle in Britain. At the time of its building in the late 13th century, it was considered a revolutionary masterpiece of military planning

1318, Despenser had Llewellyn Bren brought to Cardiff to be hanged, drawn and quartered, which only fuelled the hatred of the Welsh for Despenser. But Despenser's power at court grew until he was virtually king. During this time of power he built the Great Hall at Caerphilly Castle. Edward II's estranged wife Isabella and her lover Roger Mortimer landed a small army from France in 1326, which sent Edward and Despenser running for cover, and for a time they took refuge at Caerphilly Castle. They were eventually captured and Despenser was executed in November 1326, while Edward II was forced to abdicate.

From this turbulent time on, Caerphilly Castle's role as a fortress of national importance declined. It also declined as a domestic residence. Its successive owners, who were multiple property owners, preferred the comforts of other properties. The castle fell into ruin and its stone was quarried for buildings elsewhere.

In the nineteenth century, with the Pre-Raphaelites and the burgeoning nostalgia for the middle ages, there was a move to conserve Caerphilly Castle and protect it from further ruin. The great hall was re-roofed in the 1870s. Between 1928 and 1939 John Crichton Stuart, the fourth Marquess of Bute, undertook the restoration of Caerphilly Castle. He had many of the collapsed buildings rebuilt and restored and re-landscaped the defence works. After the castle was taken on by the state in 1950, the consolidation and restoration of the castle continued. The reflooding of the lakes was completed, and the Great Hall of Hugh Despenser was restored. Today the castle is a major tourist attraction, with a collection of massive siege engines on display.

CASTELL COCH

Castell Coch is a great Victorian masterpiece in medieval castle style. The architect William Burges created two castles for the third Marquess of Bute, one at Cardiff and the other at Castell Coch. The Butes were an old and wealthy Scottish family with estates in Wales, and they became multi-millionaires in the middle of the nineteenth century as a result of the industrial development of Cardiff. The third Marquess was fascinated by the middle ages to the point of obsession. Burges too was an obsessive medievalist, to the extent of wearing antique costumes, at least in private.

Burges's Castell Coch was built on a site with a history. It had once carried a real medieval motte-and-bailey castle, though that had been destroyed in the fifteenth century. Burges carefully followed the original ground plan, and to that extent his castle was a reconstruction. But he used grey limestone instead of the red sandstone used for the original castle. Above the ground plan, he followed his own instinct about the shapes and heights of the towers and walls. As a result he probably made the towers much higher than they had originally been, and of unequal heights, which was probably fanciful. He also gave the skyline steeply pitched roofs, which were more continental than British in style.

Castell Coch is, even so, all very impressive, including the courtyard, which has no parallels in genuine medieval castles. The well is genuine and the murder holes above the gateway are authentic. The entrance gatehouse with its drawbridge has a distinctly central European look about it. Usually gatehouses and barbicans have twin towers. Burges characteristically gave his just one, but it is massive and surprisingly tall, a great drum of masonry with a spatter of variously

sized window openings and a fine conical roof. It is a sight to make you stop and stare, which is what both William Burges and Lord Bute wanted.

William Burges died before he could get going on the interior, though he left plans and designs for it. His successors, who carried out his designs, toned them down a good deal. As a result, the inside of Castell Coch is less extravagant than Cardiff, which more truly represents Burges's work, but there are some genuine Burges touches. Lady Bute's round bedroom at the top of the main tower has a curved and domed roof. It has a great bed of state decorated with crystal balls and also an ingenious dressing-table and washstand with porcelain towers containing water. This might seem like a piece of Burges fantasy, but there was at least one genuinely medieval example, at Battle Hall in Kent.

Lord Bute loved it all. At Castell Coch in 1875, Lord Bute planted his own vineyard so that he could drink his own wine, as he imagined his medieval predecessors would have done. He perhaps unwisely asked his guests what they thought of his wine. Sir Herbert Maxwell was fairly diplomatic; 'Well now, Lord Bute, this is what I should call an interesting wine.'

Rarely used and still perfectly preserved, this Victorian extravaganza must be seen to be believed. Its servants' hall houses an exhibition about the buildings of Bute and Burges, and visitors can walk, ride or picnic in the now mature woodlands planted as a backdrop for this fairytale castle.

CARDIFF CASTLE

GLAMORGAN

The occupying Roman army established a fort at Cardiff in the first century AD, enlarging it in the fourth century. When the Normans arrived in the eleventh century and built their castle – on the same site – the remains of the Roman walls were buried under earth ramparts. This nevertheless had the virtue of preserving some stretches of Roman wall, and they were revealed during archaeological excavations in 1889. The Roman walls were rebuilt between 1922 and 1925 on their original foundations, which had survived well. This discreet remaking of history goes on unobtrusively at site after site. Few people realize that the 'Roman' city wall at Chichester is largely a much later rebuild.

The Norman castle had a motte, a round artificial mound, as its centrepiece. Initially this had a wooden tower built on top of it, but this was replaced with a stone shell keep in the twelfth century. The structure was further reinforced in the two succeeding centuries by the De Clare family who owned Cardiff Castle. In that period the keep gained a gatehouse and forebuildings that were linked by means of a massive ward wall to a new tower on the south side; this was called the Black Tower. This ward wall and the keep forebuildings were misguidedly demolished by Capability Brown during a redevelopment of the Castle site in the 1770s. The moat that surrounded the motte was also filled in at that time, though later restored; modern masonry marks the positions of the old ward wall and forebuildings taken down by Brown to make the castle more picturesque. Many landowners were building ruined castles to enhance their parks; here, Brown was selectively demolishing a castle to improve its appearance.

Richard Beauchamp, the Earl of Warwick, built a new tower and hall block on the western wall in 1423. In the late sixteenth century the Herbert family converted it into a well-appointed and luxurious house.

John Stuart, the third Marquess, was described as 'the richest baby in Britain' when he inherited Cardiff Castle and much else. He spent large sums of money on building projects at his many properties, and in 1869 he started work on the remodelling of Cardiff Castle.

The Victorian restoration of Cardiff Castle was carried out to the designs of William Burges, a committed, not to say fanatical, Gothic Revival architect. This was not so much a conservation and restoration process as a conversion of a medieval castle into a Victorian theme park. Lord Bute's great wealth enabled Burges to design and build his most fanciful schemes. The exterior was smoothed up in a restrained style, but the interior was fitted out in an ostentatious faux-medieval style. Some of the rooms are among the most remarkable ever created in the Victorian era. William Burges also rebuilt Castell Coch, not far from Cardiff, as a summer retreat for Lord Bute; this features yet more of Burges's Gothic fantasy interiors. These imaginative re-creations of the middle ages are close in spirit to King Ludwig's fantasy castle of Neuschwanstein.

INDEX